PLAY IT
SAFE

PLAY IT SAFE

KEEPING YOUR KIDS AND

YOUTH MINISTRY ALIVE

JACK CRABTREE

VICTOR BOOKS

A DIVISION OF SCRIPTURE PRESS PUBLICATIONS INC.
USA CANADA ENGLAND

ISBN 1-56476-110-X

Cover Design: Scott Rattray

1 2 3 4 5 6 7 8 9 10 Printing/Year 97 96 95 94 93

Produced by the Livingstone Corporation. David R. Veerman, J. Michael Kendrick, Kathleen Ristow, and Brenda James Todd, project staff.

Library of Congress Cataloging-in-Publication Data
Crabtree, Jack, 1949–
    p.   cm.
    1. Safety education. 2. Accidents–Prevention. 3. Church work with youth. I. Title.
HV675.C73 1993
613.6–dc20

Contents

This book is dedicated to
Jack and Mary Lu Masterson
and their family.

Thank you for the unconditional love
and support you have shown to me and
the Youth For Christ staff.

Introduction

Here's what you should know about this book:

1) ALL THE STORIES ARE TRUE! What you read in the following pages really happened to me or one of the many youth leaders who were interviewed for this book. Some of the stories are clearly identified with a real name and place. I did change the names and disguised the nonessential circumstances of some of the stories to maintain the privacy (and sometimes embarrassment!) of those who contributed to this book. When just a first name is given, the name used is fictional and is not even slightly related to the real name.

2) I'M A VIOLATOR! I'm no safety nut. You won't catch me wearing safety goggles and carrying a clip board with 99 safety check points. When the pages ahead sound preachy, remember I'm a fellow sinner in safety matters (other matters too). I'm guilty of laziness, procrastination, ego, fear, overconfidence, and all the other basic reasons we let safety slide. Preparing this material has reminded me repeatedly about how generous God has been to protect the students under my leadership when I have been poorly prepared to guard their well-being. I have a

few months head start on you, but we both have a lot of improving to do to protect the health and safety of our young people.

3) THIS BOOK IS NOT COMPLETE! No doubt you have learned or will learn additional safety lessons not included in these pages. In areas of first aid, insurance, liability, legal requirements, sexual abuse, and so on, I did my best to touch just the high points. There is so much for you to learn in each of these areas. During the next few years I believe the subject of safety and negligence in our churches will be a growing concern to all of us. I hope each of you will go much farther than this book can take you.

4) I HAD PLENTY OF HELP! My sincere thanks goes to many people who provided much needed assistance and encouragement to this project. Special thanks to: Dave Veerman, Jim Galvin, and Bruce Barton of Livingstone who conceived this idea, gave me an opportunity to develop it, and patiently guided me through the process; Claudia Gerwin, who did a zillion phone interviews with youth leaders all across the country; and Michael Kendrick whose phone calls always spurred my work.

Thanks to youth leaders and camp directors who told us their stories and shared the safety lessons they have learned: Ed Ahlum, Bob Arnold, Tim Atkins, Francis Bartley, Clarence Boland, Bob Borman, Mike Collison, Charlene Cosman, Geoff Cragg, Ken Cragg, Jon Dennis, Byron Emmert, Willie Foote, Jim Green, Betty Ham, Bill Housley, Greg Makin, Mark Miller, Greg Monaco, Mark Oestricher, Jerry Petillon, Terry Prisk, Kaaren Rexroth, John Richmond, Gary Schulte, Joel Smith, Tedd Smith, Peter Vanacore, David Wager, and Bob Kobielush, President of Christian Camping International.

Thanks to the professionals from the fields of law, counseling, social work, and insurance who discussed safety issues with me from their professional experience: Dick Armstrong, Laura Barnes, John Helfrich, Joseph Infranco, Jim Jensen, Herb Nichols, Dennis Morosco, James Murphy, and Jim Trump.

Special thanks to Becky, my wonderful wife, for her diligent proofreading, candid comments, and steadfast love to me and to Andy and Ben, my teenage sons, who give me many reasons to smile!

P.S. If you have a youth ministry safety story to tell or if this book has provoked any change in the way you do youth ministry, drop me a note. I've still got plenty to learn.

Jack Crabtree
Long Island YFC
Box 55
Deer Park, NY 11729

"He who trusts in himself is a fool, but he who walks in wisdom is kept safe" (Prov. 28:26).

CHAPTER ONE
This Shouldn't Have Happened . . .

The bad news had been delivered. It was a no-win situation. Larry, a 28-year-old youth pastor, stood in the doorway halfway between the church van full of teenagers and the desk in the canoe outfitter's shop. In all the planning for this trip he had never even considered this problem.

He stared at the swollen river on the other side of the parking lot. How was he supposed to know this was the weekend the water from the reservoir was released into the river? What was he going to do—run the river or drive this van home?

The owner of the outfitter's shop said only experienced canoeists had any business being on the river today. That warning was inside Larry's head, fighting with the fact that they had driven three hours hauling a rack of six canoes for this special one day outing. The van was rocking from side to side with the pent-up energy of teenagers psyched for a wild day running the river. Larry felt the pressure building.

Five minutes later Larry pulled the van and trailer into a parking lot a mile down the road from the outfitter's shop. He asked his crew of teenagers from the church how many of them had canoeing experience. Only the hand of his volunteer leader went up to join his. With a look of resignation and a slight laugh Larry shouted, "What are we waiting for?"

Within minutes of hitting the river almost every canoe had

capsized. Everyone was soaked and shivering in the frigid, fast-moving current. It was going to be an adventure.

Larry: Awesome Youth Leader or Stupid Fool?

Several months later the youth group was still retelling the stories of how they ran the river. Most memorable and laughable was Patty being so wet and cold she turned blue and couldn't breathe. She was shivering so much she didn't have enough strength to get out of the water and back into the canoe. It wasn't until later that night at home that she was able to get warm.

A parent overheard the conversations of the young people and approached Larry privately to express his concern. He asked Larry if he had recognized Patty's symptoms as clear signs of hypothermia and suggested Patty could have lost her life that day in the river. He questioned the decision Larry made to canoe given the condition of the river that day and the inexperience of the young people.

OBJECTIONS
Why some youth workers resist any serious safety emphasis in their youth program:
1. Nothing bad has happened to us yet.
2. You can't think of rules for everything.
3. If we follow all these safety rules, we won't be able to have any fun.
4. Relax, God will take care of us.

Larry deflected the parent's concern by assuring him no one had gotten hurt. More important was the fact the teens had a great time. Adventure and a few risks make the youth group exciting and more attractive to the nonchurched teens that attend. Driving home would have hurt the positive image of the youth group. Larry added he was confident God would protect them from any real danger. They have people in the church praying for the youth ministry. It would have been a big mistake if he had driven them home without going in the river.

Larry continued his youth ministry not giving another thought to the incident. Most of the students in the youth group still think Larry is an awesome youth leader. Fortunately, for Patty's sake, Larry didn't learn his safety lesson the hard way. Unfortunately, Larry hasn't learned his safety lesson at all. He just keeps rolling along.

Don't think badly of Larry. He does care about his students

and would never want to see any of them hurt. To him, discussion of safety concerns is boring and stifles the freedom and fun he promotes in the youth ministry activities. Safety warnings sound restricting and probably would squash the excitement and spontaneous fun the youth group is supposed to have.

Larry can't picture himself standing before his youth group reading off a list of safety regulations. Nothing would destroy the atmosphere of his group as fast as a safety lecture. It would make him sound like a parent. Fear and caution are signs of "thinking old." Larry prides himself in "thinking young."

Larry's attitude toward safety issues reflects the attitudes and practices of many youth ministry workers—both paid employees of the church or organization and volunteers. Safety is one of the last concerns discussed as youth activities are planned and implemented.

What if Patty Had Died?

Consider the consequences of a different outcome of Patty's time in that chilly river. Suppose the hypothermia had advanced a few more degrees. Patty would have stopped breathing and her heart would have stopped beating. How prepared was Larry to respond to this life or death crisis?

Imagine that the best efforts of the ambulance team and the hospital were not enough to save Patty's life. How would it affect all the people involved?

1) Grief, sorrow and shock would ravage the youth group and the church.

2) Heartbreak and deep sadness would hammer her family, her boyfriend, and best friends. They would cry out to God about why such a fine young woman had to die before reaching the fulfilling years of her life.

3) Eventually anger and blame would be leveled at Larry and the volunteer leader. The story of raising hands in the van would be public knowledge. People would second-guess Larry and condemn his decision to canoe the river.

4) New, strong love-hate feelings would surface in the youth group. In one sense the tragedy would give them reason to

comfort each other with deeper feelings than ever before. However, the painful memories of Patty's death would make it hard to be together without that experience being foremost in their minds. It is likely many members would seek escape and reduce their involvement.

5) Personal guilt would weigh heavy on Larry, the volunteer leader, and any student or adult who felt responsible for what happened to Patty. Larry's personal effectiveness and work habits would likely suffer for an extended period of time. He would find it hard to concentrate for any length of time because his thoughts would keep returning to what happened that day on the river.

6) Within a month, the church leadership would conduct some kind of review concerning the accident. Larry's leadership and his present effectiveness would be closely reviewed. Parents would voice concerns about safety issues in all aspects of the youth program. Regardless of the outcome, Larry's status would be diminished in the eyes of the church leaders and the parents of the students involved.

7) Most likely, Larry and the church could expect some type of lawsuit related to Patty's death. The proceedings would continue for several years. The litigation would provoke rifts between all the people involved. The whole tragic story would have to be retold many times during the judicial process. There would be plenty of hard feelings between everyone involved on the issues of responsibility, pain, negligence, and money. This day on the river, it seems, would never go away.

8) No one would come out of this chain of events untouched. Everyone would be changed. Relationships would change. Attitudes would change. The personal Christian faith of some would grow stronger; others would feel their faith shaken and fall away from their commitment to Christ and the church.

9) One constant would remain. Patty would be gone. What happened couldn't be undone.

For years Larry would reexamine his motives for taking Patty and the group into the river on that fateful day. He would have to admit to himself that he never thought about the possibility of someone dying that day. When he made his decision, he was thinking about wasting a three-hour van ride and listening to the complaints of students who would question his "awesome" status as a leader if he talked safety and decided not to canoe.

Eventually Larry might have thought of a creative alternate plan he could have used on that day if he had said no to canoeing. Unfortunately, on the day of the accident those thoughts never crossed his mind.

Of course Larry's attention to safety issues would be changed forever. He would have learned the safety lesson from the most severe teacher—the tragic experience.

Changing Attitudes toward Safety

Interviews with numerous youth workers reveal the major reasons for a significant change in attitude toward safety issues. They were asked to complete the sentence, "I never took safety seriously until. . . ." Their responses included the following:

". . . I got older and had children of my own."

". . . I saw a student in my group get seriously hurt."

". . . a friend in youth ministry was involved in a horrible lawsuit over an accident involving the youth group."

> "Carelessness is a popular way to hate a kid in the Christian ministry. If you love someone, you don't do a careless job on safety. Carelessness will undermine your goal of bringing them to Christ and establishing them in the church."
> *Jerry Petillon*
> 10-year youth ministry veteran in Detroit

". . . some parents asked me why I hadn't done something to stop the game in which a student was seriously hurt."

". . . my board of advisors talked to me about our legal liability."

". . . after a close call where we escaped a serious injury, I realized how careless we had been."

". . . I got hurt myself during a retreat."

Youth workers who have learned the importance of safety in the ministry identify five major reasons why they were previously unconcerned.

I Was Young. Young leaders feel indestructible. They believe nothing can hurt them. Challenges are to be taken, not analyzed. The younger the youth worker, the less likely he or she is to be adequately concerned about safety.

Young leaders don't have to give up their enthusiasm and energy, but when they face safety issues, they must force themselves to think like a person who has lived a few more years than their kids.

I Had No Children. Parents seem overly cautious and careful until a young leader becomes a parent. Having a child sharpens a person's awareness of danger and safety. One important role of a parent is to think ahead and anticipate any potentially harmful situations. Parents "childproof" a room to keep children from encountering what could possibly hurt them. The responsible youth leader thinks the same way as he or she prepares for the youth group meeting. It's a mindset more naturally embraced by a parent who daily looks after his or her own children.

I Wanted Kids to Like Me. No youth leader wants to spend every activity or trip saying no to the kids in the group. Not wanting to offend or drive away a young person, youth leaders are sometimes afraid to confront students involved in dangerous activities. The mature youth leader knows students are not offended when they are confronted in a personal, affirming encounter. Students don't want to be yelled at or condemned in front of their peers, but they do appreciate a respectful call to responsibility and maturity.

I Couldn't Afford It. Preparing to operate a safety-conscious youth ministry costs time and money. Most youth workers are running their program on a last-minute schedule either because they are procrastinators or volunteers in a time squeeze. They rarely consider safety issues. Many times events and activities are planned with no thought given to the potential dangers present. Safety requires training of leaders in specific subjects (such as first aid, water safety, and emergency procedures) that require a significant time commitment. How many youth leaders are willing to invest the time and money for such training?

I Had No Experience. A few trips to the hospital emergency room or visits to the hospital room of a student injured during a youth group activity will change a leader's attitude toward safety. Nothing beats firsthand experience. Unfortunately, it is a painful and costly method of learning. Wisdom can also be gained by watching others and heeding the warnings and advice of those who have paid the price of actual experience. Pride and stubbornness, however, keep some people from learning by any other method than their own failures. It's a heavy price to pay.

Carrying Precious Cargo

Bob had an eye-opening experience during his first year as youth minister for the church. "I was driving a vanload of students from my church to YFC's DC '91. Just outside of Washington D.C., I noticed the brakes were almost totally gone. I pushed the brake pedal all the way to the floor with little response.

"We were already late so I took it real slow and nursed the van the last 10 miles with no brakes into the downtown convention center. We arrived safely, and I thought of myself as a hero for getting us through that tough spot.

"A year later I wonder how I could have been so stupid. I had no idea what the terrain of the road or the traffic would be. I could have easily gotten the van into the situation where only a crash would have stopped us.

"I realize now that my response to that crisis matches the way I have handled personal car problems during my life. The difference this time was that I was no longer just responsible for me. I had 13 kids who belonged to someone else with me but were under my supervision and protection.

"I now realize when I operate as youth minister, I must do what parents and the church would want me to do, not what I personally feel comfortable doing."

Bob has had a key attitude transformation in his youth ministry. Now he is aware that in addition to his important job of communicating the Christian message to young people, he is also responsible for providing a safe, responsible environment. His role as youth minister requires him to answer to several important groups of people who will hold him accountable for his decisions.

A youth leader must be able to give satisfactory answers to the key questions from the people who have put their trust in him as he works with their kids.

The parents want to know:

- Are you protecting my children from danger and harm?
- Do you model a responsible lifestyle for my kids?
- Are you teaching my kids to make good decisions?
- Do you think through all the activities before you ask my son or daughter to participate?
- Do you love my kids enough to say "no" to them when it is necessary?

The sponsoring church/organization wants to know:

- Are you being a witness for Christ to everyone involved by showing care and concern for each person's safety?
- Will your actions bring sorrow to people under our care
- Are you teaching and modeling maturity to our youth?
- Are you exposing us to any unwise liability?
- Will you bring us any bad publicity?

The participating students want to know:

- Will you carelessly hurt my friends?
- Will you pressure me to take chances I cannot handle?
- Are you concerned about my future?
- Am I going to have sad memories because of a careless accident?

The insurance carrier wants to know:

- Is our contract with your group a wise investment?
- Will you follow the rules and restrictions we specify?
- Will you do your job as our partner in protecting these young people?

Pretend you are our friend, Larry, the awesome youth leader. If Patty had died that day in the river, how would you answer these questions? Let the words come out of your mouth so you can hear how they will sound to the ears of those who will ask the questions.

Don't skip ahead! Try to answer for Larry all the questions these people will ask him.

If it is hard to find the right words, make a promise to yourself to never let careless planning or thoughtless decisions put you in that position. Use all the information in this book to reform your youth ministry into an operation which is both fun and safe. Be committed to giving your students thrilling memories and a lifetime relationship with Jesus, while protecting their physical well-being.

Fun Or Safety?

For most youth ministries, fun is the major drawing card for attracting students to attend. Not many students are attracted to a youth group because it is safe. It would seem that any group emphasizing safety will seem boring and could expect a drop in attendance.

Just consider the connotations that *fun* and *safety* carry for most young people and their leaders.

Fun Means . . .	Safety Means . . .
saying yes to kids	saying no to kids
kids like the leader	leader unpopular with kids
risk, danger, excitement	rules, caution, boredom
yes! go for it!	no! don't try it!
have a good time	checklists
never being bored	chaperones, counselors
freedom	supervision
funny stories to tell	oppressive adult presence
spontaneity	worry and paranoia
living by faith	excessive caution

Many youth workers falsely assume that being safe means not

having much fun. Deep in their minds they think if they decide to run a safe youth program, it probably won't be much fun or be effective reaching kids today.

Surprisingly, safe programs can still be plenty of fun. It does take extra planning and recruiting more qualified people to make activities both fun and safe, but the leader can be confident that the fun of the ministry won't come to an abrupt halt because of a serious injury which could have been prevented with proper planning.

Carelessness is sometimes just the result of laziness. Searching for fun activities, leaders grab the first good idea they find without giving it a thorough safety examination. A few minor changes or adjustments can turn a risky game into a safe one without reducing the level of fun.

You can do the best possible job of planning and protecting and still see students get injured or even killed. There are many forces you cannot control. Your responsibility is to recognize the forces you do control and make them safe for the young people you love.

CHAPTER TWO
How Safe Is Your Youth Ministry?

It's Friday night. You're the adult leader of the church youth ministry. To give your students something positive to do this weekend night, you decide to open the church gym and the youth room. No program. No planning. No problems. Right?

The lights are on. The basketballs are bouncing in the gym. The television and VCR are playing in the youth room. Teens are scattered throughout the lighted section of the church. You opened the church at 7 P.M. and will use your key to close it up a 11:30 P.M. Everything seems fine.

Stop and think! What potential risks or dangers await a youth leader who is just trying to help teenagers by simply opening the church for a night of recreation and hanging out? Here's a list of some of the potentially dangerous situations that might occur during this "harmless" night of youth activity at the church. Check the floor plan of the church (on the next page) and the appropriate numbers linked with the potential problems.

Risk 1: You Are Alone. None of the other volunteer leaders could make it tonight. What would you do if a student needed emergency transportation to the hospital or home? Are you vulnerable to a false accusation of abuse by a student without another adult present? Who would take charge if *you* were injured tonight?

Risk 2: Open Door Policy. The kids in your group can walk in and out without asking your permission. You have no written record of who is actually here. Two blocks away is a pizza parlor where they like to go for a quick snack. You have never had someone leave and not come back. Will tonight be any different?

Risk 3: Excitement in the Parking Lot. Kids rush out into the parking lot to see another student's new car. You can hear the motor revving and the short squeal of the tires. They love to drive in circles with other kids sitting on the hood. Should you step outside and play the meanie?

Risk 4: Action in the Gym. The basketball game is only half court, but they are playing hard. You notice the protective mat for the wall under the backboard is missing. There are a couple rectangular tables with metal protected edges left from the ladies luncheon still set up inside the boundary lines of the court. You know you would hear plenty of groaning if you stopped the game to fix all these situations.

THE COMMON SAFETY SINS OF YOUTH MINISTRY

1. Not enough staff
2. Too many kids in the vehicle
3. No time to plan for safety
4. No plan of action to respond to an emergency
5. Students driving
6. No use of seat belts
7. No first aid training or supplies
8. Inadequate paperwork (proper permission/medical forms)
9. Letting a dangerous activity continue (afraid to stop it)
10. Lack of careful supervision (letting kids wander or play around with equipment)

Risk 5: Michael Jordan Wannabes. At the other end of the basketball court some kids are trying to dunk the basketball by jumping off a metal folding chair as they run toward the basket. Each time they jump the chair moves. They are falling on the floor and laughing hysterically. You will have a hard time convincing them somebody could get hurt.

Risk 6: Young Lovers. You have two steady boy-girl couples who are always hanging on to each other. Where are they now? Are they in the youth room watching videos or have they wandered down a dark hallway into another section of the church? Should you go looking for them?

Risk 7: The Video Tape. The television tube is the only light in the youth room. It is hard to see who is bunched into all the couches staring at the screen. One of the students brought the video. You can hear the gunfire and some of the bad language. Should you be monitoring what they watch on these nights?

Risk 8: The Ride Home. A cute tenth-grade girl tells you she is leaving now with some friends who will take her home. Should you let her go? And who are these "friends" waiting for her with the car keys in their hands? You never saw them before. When did they arrive? You know questioning her about all this will make her feel uncomfortable in front of these friends. She assures you her parents won't mind.

Risk 9: Who You Gonna Call? There is a telephone in the church office. Unfortunately it is locked and you don't have that key. If someone were seriously hurt, how would you call for help? If you did get help or had to go to the hospital, would they treat the student if they could not reach the parents tonight, since you have no permission slip or release form for this activity?

Risk 10: The Drive Home. If you have to drive some of the kids home tonight, is your insurance coverage sufficient to cover the medical and liability costs for a carload of teenagers if you were in an accident? What should you do if the last person in the car is a student of the opposite sex? If someone spread a rumor about your romantic involvement with a student, or if a student accused you of a sexual advance, what recourse or protection would you have?

Should We Always Be Afraid?

Does the risk list make you permanently paranoid? The list of possible risks is endless. Do you consider this a ridiculous attack of fearful speculation or is there an element of hidden, but real risk every time you offer a youth ministry event?

All of us live with risks and danger every day. Just driving a car reminds us how close we come to serious injury or death. Just a few inches or seconds could mean the difference between life and death. Most of us have to admit that we have been fortunate when we have had lapses in our driving safety. Nothing serious happened. However if we ignore these little safety "wake up" calls, eventually we will pay for it.

We can dismiss this safety check as extreme or take it seriously. However, there are risks in becoming safety conscious. It may affect your popularity. Will becoming safety-conscious transform you into a youth leader who is no longer fun to be around? Will kids stop coming to your youth ministry if you make safety a priority?

The risk of being a youth leader in North America has increased greatly in the past 10 years. While the value of each young life has remained priceless, the legal and monetary damages involved have skyrocketed. The youth leader who overlooks the crucial role of safety in his or her ministry risks substantial losses in ministry opportunities, relationships, reputation, time, and finances.

Becoming a Student of Safety

Most likely you weren't selected to be a leader in youth ministry because you had a reputation as being safety conscious. You were selected because kids like you or because you know how to have a good time while communicating the Gospel. But everyone connected with your youth ministry is quietly counting on you to run a safe program and take care of their kids.

It's okay to admit that safety is not one of your major concerns or strengths as a leader. Just the fact that you are reading this shows your openness to starting from where you are and learning how you can grow as a youth leader who understands safety concerns.

Let's be honest. Safety is a background concern. It's like being an offensive lineman in football. No one notices anything you do until a defensive player gets by you to slam the quarterback into the ground. Then all eyes focus on you, and everyone asks why you didn't do your job. Learn this lesson now. Seldom will anyone discuss safety with you until something goes wrong and someone gets hurt. Unfortunately, learning your lesson then won't get a kid out of a wheelchair or bring someone back from the grave.

Safety is a huge assumption that everyone makes about youth ministry. The people who hired you assume you will be safe and not hurt any of the young people. The students assume nothing bad will ever happen to them and their friends. You assume God is with you and will protect you from harm.

Requirements for Students of Safety

First, a youth leader needs to be personally committed to safety. How will you be transformed into a safety-conscious person? Will it start as fear of liability, or as fear of what you would tell a parent on the phone if his or her son or daughter were seriously injured or even killed while under your supervision? Although fear is a powerful motivator, youth leaders should take safety measures primarily because they have a strong love for all the students involved.

You don't want to see anyone get hurt. Your commitment to safety means investing time to think ahead and planning a response to possible dangerous situations. It takes initiative. It's proactive, not reactive. This investment also requires money and people. The student of safety rejects the shortcut approach. It is worth the money to purchase quality equipment and hire skilled people to provide expertise for training and medical response.

Second, the student of safety is constantly improving his ability to assess risk and danger. That ability is gained only through experience. You can learn vicariously by reading the true stories in this book and listening to others. Or you can learn through real-life experiences. You pack away knowledge for future use every time you lead a youth activity or trip. You hope and pray to learn all the important safety lessons without seeing some young people lose their health or their life.

Developing this risk-assessment skill is like learning to drive a car. If you are smart, you start cautiously, learning to control and stop the car. The fools and the reckless hit the accelerator and think about how to stop safely only when it is too late and the damage is done. It is not a sin to err on the side of caution. Every activity and event you conduct broadens your safety and ministry experience and equips you for more demanding opportunities.

Principles of Safety

The remaining chapters of this book provide specific examples and instruction for common youth ministry experiences. No book can address all the situations you will face, but every student of safety can master the following general safety principles and apply them in varied settings.

1. The Higher the Risk, the Greater the Supervision Required. Meetings each week in the church youth room require a 1:15 adult leader-to-student ratio. But a weekend hike in the wilderness probably requires a 1:4 ratio. Raking leaves at the home of a senior citizen may require a 1:10 ratio, while handing out bag lunches to the homeless in an inner city setting may call for a 1:2 ratio.

2. What Is Dangerous? Get a Clue! The exclusions of coverage by your insurance company give a general guideline for what the underwriters consider dangerous. Most liability policies presently exclude snowmobiling, mud bowls, water balloon launchers, and whitewater rafting. Those exclusions are made on the basis of previous accidents. Obviously activities which involve motorized vehicles, slippery surfaces, heavy physical contact, turbulent water, and hitting people with any type of projectile deserve special attention before you decide to proceed with your plans.

3. Perceived Danger versus Actual Danger. There is a big difference. You can keep the atmosphere of fun and excitement in your youth program if you sponsor activities which look and feel dangerous, but in fact are quite safe. A ropes course (i.e., walking a single wire 20 feet off the ground) is both terrifying and thrilling to most students. In reality, a well-maintained and well-run ropes course is one of the safest experiences a young person can have because of the ever-present safety lines and high quality supervision. On the other hand, most adults and students feel relaxed and complacent about safety around water when in fact the danger is much higher than they suspect (85 percent of all fatal accidents in the wilderness involve water).

Alan had the greatest job. Here he was in his mid 20s playing basketball in a small church gym with a group of guys from his YFC/Campus Life club. Spending time building relationships with these guys was what his boss wanted him to do.

He broke loose from his man and bolted toward the basket. On the way he tripped on the foot of another player, lost his balance, stumbled and crashed into the unpadded wall underneath the backboard. He laid on the floor motionless while the teenage guys stared at him in shock.

Today Alan is living a productive life as an inner-city worker for the Presbyterian church, but when he moves he does it in a wheelchair. He has been paralyzed since that fateful day of basketball.

If you had come to a gym to play basketball or a similar game and saw no padded protective mats on the walls, what decision would you make?

4. Plan for the Worst-Case Scenario. The best training (prior to an actual experience) is discussing potential problem situations. Example: As you train counselors and drivers for the winter retreat, ask them what they would do if their van (with 10 students) was separated from the rest of the caravan and developed engine problems. If they were 10 miles from the nearest town, it was nighttime, and it was five degrees above zero, how would they handle the situation? Example: In training leaders for your summer bike trip, ask what would they do if they realized they had made a wrong turn on the route and were 10 miles from the destination. It is almost dark. What should they do? Help them think through all their options and prepare them to make decisions when the real life events occur.

5. Learn to Recognize the Initial Signs of Danger. Great athletes have the ability to anticipate what their opponent is going to do next. Responding more quickly than their foes can act, they gain the victory. The safety-smart youth leader anticipates danger. If students are chicken fighting (riding on each other's shoulders) in the small swimming pool, can you see the probable landing spot for the head of the student riding on top when he or she falls? What are the signs that two young men are growing angry at each other during a competitive game and may begin using excessive force during the next round? Recognizing the initial signs of danger gives the youth leader the advantage to intervene before the accident happens.

6. Keep in Mind the Special Needs of Your Group. Learn to make safety decisions according to the particular needs of the kids in your group. If you take your group on a follow-the-leader exercise through the park, you may jump over a wrought iron fence without realizing that down the line is a student who is overweight and could be injured trying to get over the fence. Putting your pint-sized junior high students in a heavy physical contact game with your senior highers usually brings trouble.

7. Test It First. Bring your great idea to life with a simulated run, using your staff as "crash test dummies." As you play, you will be able to identify the danger points and make changes before you present it to the youth group.

8. Resist the Shortcuts. Recognize the forces that pressure you to shortcut your safety plans. When you are running late, you will tend to skip checking the fluids in the van or the connections on the ropes course. People will forget permission slips, first aid kits, etc. Don't let their "problem" pressure you to break the important rules of safety.

9. Make the Most of Your Mistakes. Learn from your mistakes and the mistakes of others. Minor accidents or near misses are sometimes funny. But don't just laugh about them. Learn your lesson and believe that next time you might not be so fortunate.

10. Take the "My Kid" Test. Treat each young person like your own child. Don't put any student in a situation in which you would not readily place your own child.

11. Lead by Example. The leader sets the pace for the volunteers in the issues of safety and every other matter in youth ministry. Don't bend the rules for your personal comfort or convenience.

12. Balance Your Theology. Pray for God's protection, but exercise the thoughtful responsibility God has given to you.

Don't count on Him to suspend the forces of nature and the laws of physics to protect you from the results of careless planning.

Teach these general principles of safety to your team of volunteer youth workers. Share experiences which illustrate these principles and discuss how they apply to your group.

Wake Up and Smell the Coffee!

All youth leader need to do an honest, thorough assessment of safety issues in their ministry to protect themselves, the reputation of their church or youth organization, and the well-being of the students and families whom they love and serve. Answer the following questions to focus on the vital safety issues in your youth ministry.

How Safe Is Your Youth Ministry?
Volunteer Leaders
(Check One)

Yes	Sometimes	No	The Questions
			Have my volunteer leaders gone through an application and acceptance process (including written applications, reference forms, background checks, and interviews)?
			Have my volunteer leaders been screened for any criminal, sexual, or physical abuse accusations or violations in their past?
			Have my volunteer leaders been trained for the job I have asked them to do?
			Have I trained them in general safety procedures, and do I discuss specific safety procedures with them prior to an activity or event?

Yes	Sometimes	No	The Questions
			Are my volunteers aware of and do they practice our prescribed standard of "safe conduct" with students to avoid any suspicion of sexual misconduct?
			Do my volunteers know their job at the events they attend?
			Do I have an appropriate adult-student ratio at the events?

Student Information
(Check One)

Yes	Sometimes	No	The Questions
			Do I have a permission/release form and medical form signed by parent(s) and notarized for each participating student?
			Do I have current phone numbers to get in touch with parents in case of an emergency?
			Are parents fully informed (in writing) about the activities in which their children will be involved?
			If I have to take any of these students to the hospital, am I prepared to answer the questions I will be asked about their personal information, medical information, and insurance?

First Aid and Emergency Response
(Check One)

Yes	Sometimes	No	The Questions
			Are the members of my youth ministry team trained in a certified first aid course?
			Is a person trained in first aid present at all of our youth activities and trips?
			Is our first aid kit adequately stocked and available at all of our youth activities and trips?
			Do I carry with me phone numbers of important people who should be contacted in case of an emergency (ambulance, police, ministry supervisor, parents, etc.)?

Drivers and Vehicles
(Check One)

Yes	Sometimes	No	The Questions
			Do we have a written policy on driving standards and who is allowed to drive for all the activities and trips?
			Do we only use drivers who are qualified and responsible?
			Do we prohibit students to drive other students to our activities?
			Do we require the use of seat belts?
			Do we regularly check for safety the vehicles we use (fluids, brakes, tires, etc.)?

Planning and Preparedness

(Check One)

Yes	Sometimes	No	The Questions
			Do we have a clear written set of basic safety rules for the activities of our youth ministry?
			Do we have sufficient insurance coverage for both the leaders and students in our youth ministry?
			In preparing for an event, do I inspect the physical facilities or location and look for any safety hazards?
			In preparing for an event, do I walk through the proposed activities to anticipate what risks are involved?
			Do I think through a worst-case scenario to identify potential problems and plan responses to the problems?
			When an activity appears to be dangerous, do I have the wisdom and courage to stop it regardless of the reaction of the students involved?

Analysis: Each "no" or "sometimes" answer needs your attention. Review these questions and answers with your supervisors and your volunteer staff. Decide together what you can do to improve the protection you provide for the students in your youth ministry.

CHAPTER THREE
Are You Protected?

"Young man, how many times has your outfit been sued?" The county policeman's voice was gruff as his face locked on mine.

"None, sir," I answered timidly.

"Well, you ought to consider yourself real lucky based on what I can see of how you operate," he replied as he returned to his clip board and the paper work for our emergency call.

He had responded to our call for help when a young woman complained of severe head pains and dizziness after hitting her head during our outdoor games event with 400 teenagers in the county park. The policeman had handled our situation skillfully when he arrived minutes before the ambulance. We, however, had not won his approval with our unprofessional preparation.

We had answered almost all of his questions about this young woman with responses of "I don't know" or "I'll ask if someone here knows." We had no parental release form, health history form, or information about how to contact her parents. Our activity was just a one-day, four-hour event with students from all the Campus Life clubs in the county. The thought of having all that paperwork for just a four-hour event seemed like an unnecessary hassle.

Handing me a copy of his report in the lobby of the emergency room, the policeman sighed and shook his head. He didn't have to say any more. I heard him loud and clear. It was time to tighten up the way we ran our ministry events.

Threats to Your Youth Ministry

"Accidents in youth ministry aren't just probable; they're inevitable," says David Wager, director of Silver Birch Ranch in northern Wisconsin. "Despite our best efforts to prevent them, accidents will happen. The challenge for us is to be trained and prepared to deal with them so we can save a life."

Wager believes there is a mentality among some religious people that stresses trusting in God and hoping accidents won't happen. Consequently, many times religious people are the least prepared with practical training and skills to respond to an emergency.

In addition to lack of proper training, Wager lists the possibility of sexual abuse by staff, the lack of proper permission and health forms, and the substandard condition of vehicles and drivers used for youth ministry as major threats to the safety and credibility of a youth ministry. Often safety problems reflect economic struggles. Some Christians are reluctant to pay for what really needs to be done to make the youth ministry safe. They don't think they can afford the time or money to send their staff through a certified first-aid program, to repair and maintain their vehicles, or to buy the insurance coverage needed to protect the young people under their care.

YOU NEED PROFESSIONAL HELP

The information concerning legal matters, insurance coverage, and permission forms are extremely important to the solid foundation of your youth ministry. The material presented in this chapter is not comprehensive or intended to be used as the sole counsel for the decisions your youth ministry makes on these important topics.

Each youth minister should find an attorney and an insurance agent who are qualified and knowledgeable in these subjects as they relate to youth ministry. Incorporate these professionals into the decision-making process of your ministry. Use their knowledge and skill to design policies of operation and insurance coverage that are appropriate to your local community.

A small, summer camp organization ran a great program for young people each year. The leaders of the camp provided much of the money for its operation out of their personal finances. When faced with the choice between spending $1,800 on additional insurance coverage or purchasing new canoes and sports equipment, they opted for the canoes. A year later, after a young man was killed during a camp activity, a lawsuit was brought against the camp and the leaders. They were judged to have been negligent and were ordered to pay damages far beyond the insurance coverage they carried. They lost the camp property, and several leaders had to pay large sums out of their own pockets. The ministry of that camp was halted because they chose not to purchase the additional insurance.

The threat of legal action against churches and youth organizations is increasing. There is a growth in litigation on all fronts as people seek damages from those they accuse of harming them. People are less hesitant to bring lawsuits against churches. In some states, legislatures have amended laws to remove some of the legal protection churches and other non-profit organizations have had against lawsuits. Accidents and injuries are inevitable, and so are lawsuits. Youth ministries must be prepared.

Negligence and the Law

Negligence is "an unintentional breach of a legal duty causing damage reasonably foreseeable without which breach the damage would not have occurred." In lay terms, a youth leader has the responsibility to lead the young people under his or her charge and to make decisions about safety that any reasonable person would do to avoid danger. If a person is injured because the youth leader did not exhibit those safeguards, the leader is negligent and held responsible for any mishap.

Legally, the following tests are used to determine if negligence has occurred.

1. A Duty—an obligation recognized by the law requiring a person to conform to a certain standard of conduct for the protection of others against unreasonable risks.

2. The Act—a failure on the part of such person to conform to the standard required.

3. Proximate Cause—a reasonably close causal connection between the conduct (failure to conform to appropriate standard) and the resulting injury.

4. Damages—actual loss or damage to the interests of another.

To establish that a defendant is negligent, thus allowing the injured plaintiff to recover damages, all four elements must be proven. To establish that the defendant is not negligent, it needs to be shown that only one of the tests was not met.

The standard of care the law requires is not absolute safety, but rather reasonable actions in view of the probability of injury to others. Whether you are negligent depends upon how you acted. The standard of care required is measured by comparing it to what a person of ordinary prudence (care or caution in a sensible way) would exercise under similar circumstances. A reasonably prudent person demonstrates the sensible caution and care the people of a community would expect a normal person to exercise. Negligence is the failure to exercise that degree of care which is reasonable under the circumstances.

An additional important consideration in establishing negligence is foreseeability. If in the eyes of reasonable people an occurrence cannot be anticipated, a leader cannot be held responsible to provide protection against it. Negligence is based upon those unintentional acts that harm someone. The leader did not want the incident or the subsequent consequences to happen, but in fact the consequences could have been foreseen by a reasonable and prudent person. Such a person, it follows, would have taken precautions. The reason for failure to foresee the consequences,

WHY PARENTS SUE

1. **Surprise!** The parents had no idea that when their kids went on a youth event they would be doing the activity in which they were injured.

2. **Lack of communication.** When the youth group leaders seem unavailable or uncooperative in providing information about an event or after a young person is injured, the parents' anger rises.

3. **Wrong Decisions.** If parents feel a mistake was made by the leaders in planning or allowing a certain activity, they might sue to change the way decisions are made about youth group activities or their supervision.

4. **Covering Up.** When parents sense that an organization or a leader is withholding information or trying to transfer blame, they may become angry enough to sue.

5. **Young Leaders.** When young leaders are the primary staff of an activity where an accident occurs, parents can jump to the immediate conclusion that their child was not supervised by a capable leader.

whether it be carelessness, bad judgment, excitement, simple inattention, inexperience, ignorance, stupidity, or forgetfulness is immaterial, even though the leader was acting in good faith. The "reasonable and prudent professional" must be able to foresee from the circumstances a danger to the participant, a danger that presents an "unreasonable risk of harm" against which the participant must be protected.

The subject of liability and negligence is beyond the scope of this book. These concerns should be discussed with a local attorney trained in this area of law. Additional information can be obtained from books on legal liability, negligence, and risk management.

For a comprehensive summary of court rulings on lawsuits related to youth activities and recreation, see the three-volume set *Legal Liability and Risk Management for Public and Private Entities* by Betty van der Smissen (Anderson Press, 1990).

It isn't necessary to be a law student to have a basic understanding of negligence and the standards by which a youth leader will be judged. The purpose of this book is to motivate youth leaders to assess their programs to determine if they are inside the boundaries of "reasonable action." The true stories contained in each chapter can help a youth leader develop a higher degree of "foreseeability" as he or she plans activities and events.

Insurance Protection

What coverage should a church or youth organization consider?

Commercial General Liability. This type of insurance protects you in case of a lawsuit where negligence is charged. It also provides legal defense to protect the organization and any individuals named in a lawsuit. Despite strict safety practices, most organizations will be sued at some point in time. In today's North American society it is virtually inevitable.

The amount of general liability coverage a church or organization should carry may vary according to the size of its operation, the amount of exposure (that is, the number of activities and students involved), and geographic location. Although it is difficult to define a rule of thumb for the amount of coverage needed, a minimum starting figure is $1 million. Any amount less than $1 million is not realistic today and would not go very far if, for instance, the church van had an accident in which two youth passengers were killed and six others were seriously injured. Insurance agents agree that a church can't buy too much insurance for the coverage of young people and youth activities. Emotions run high and strong when young people are injured or killed. After a tragic accident, everyone wishes they had more coverage.

Decisions concerning coverage should be made in consultation with a reputable insurance agent. The agent can help a church or organization determine its potential liability and what kind of premiums it can afford. Many youth ministry organizations presently carry from $2 million (with a $5 million excess policy) on the low end to $25 million on the high end.

Liability insurance most often pays for the injuries and damages suffered by people we know and care about, not for strangers who are trying to get rich by suing us. Usually our coverage will be used to help the families and students for whom we conduct the youth ministry. If they are involved in a serious injury, why should they be shortchanged by our lack of planning and our failure to provide adequate coverage?

A major exclusion on most general liability policies is sexual misconduct by staff (paid and volunteer). This problem is gaining increasing publicity as more and more young people are willing to come forward with charges against the adults who have abused them. This is discussed under staff selection and supervision in chapter 4.

Activities Medical Insurance. This is an accident/sickness policy that can be purchased to handle medical bills incurred by students injured in ministry activities. This coverage can handle the immediate expenses and prevent the families from going into litigation to recover medical bills. Most families have medical insurance coverage. It should be noted on the parent's information and release form that their insurance will be used as the primary coverage in case of an injury. For most families, the youth ministry accident policy will be used as a back-up for what their primary coverage does not handle.

Because there are families that do not have medical insurance, the youth ministry or church can arrange special event insurance for one day or a weekend or for youth ministry activities throughout the year for a nominal fee ($1–2 per person for each event). It is best to build the cost of the insurance into the price of the activity. The youth ministry can buy the policy for the whole group. Insurance companies offering this type of coverage want to know the number of young people covered, not a list of names stating who wants the coverage and who doesn't. When an injury occurs, the youth ministry pays the bills of families who don't have personal medical insurance. The youth ministry then submits the bills to the insurance company for reimbursement.

Automobile Liability. Coverage is needed for hired vehicles and owned autos (suggested amount—$500,000). Drivers need to be screened carefully for their motor vehicle record and should be required to carry adequate liability coverage (suggested amount: $100,000 / $300,000) on their personal vehicles if they are ever allowed to drive any students. Vehicle safety and insurance is discussed in more detail in chapter 5.

Workers' Compensation. Requirements for workman's compensation vary from state to state. Some have lower requirements or exemptions for churches. In some states, the number of employees determines an organization's liability to provide workman's compensation. Other states have a statewide fund that handles it. Although not a widely known fact, workman's compensation does apply to volunteer workers as well as paid employees. Staff who are hurt while on the job (for instance, playing basketball at a retreat) might be covered for a work-related injury. Check with a local insurance agent to determine your exposure and responsibility.

Additional Insurance. Coverage for watercraft, aircraft, other equipment, and activities excluded from the general liability policy can be obtained on an event-by-event basis if an exposure exists. The cost of the premiums will be high. Also, liability for counseling/omissions and errors coverage is recommended for professional counselors. Youth workers who counsel informally as part of their other activities usually are protected through the church or organization's general liability policy.

Health and Liability Release Forms

Are those pieces of paper with parent's signatures worthless and a waste of time or are they valuable and necessary? Most youth workers with a few years of experience have at least one release-form story to tell. Maybe they received treatment at a hospital where they were told the paper was worthless and wanted to talk with the parents by phone before beginning treatment. But when they visit another hospital for treatment, they might find a contrasting procedure and attitude.

Health and liability release forms can be a valuable tool to protect everyone in youth ministry. Using them also helps you provide the best care for students involved in the youth ministry program. In an emergency, a signed health form might make the difference between a student receiving immediate care or having to wait until a family member is contacted. Having a complete medical history gives the hospital staff immediate medical information that may speed their ability to make a correct diagnosis and treatment. Having complete factual information about students, their families, and their insurance assists you in completing the extensive information forms used in most hospitals.

You can create your own forms. When completed by the student, the sample form provided in the appendix will give you the information needed for most comprehensive medical information and liability release forms. Review the form you decide to use with a local attorney and medical personnel from a local hospital. They will help you address any particular topic of information required in your local situation.

Helpful Tips for Using Medical and Release Forms

Keep in mind that adult staff need to complete forms too. Their medical and family information will be needed if they are injured. Every form should be completed legibly and in ink. Printing is best. Make duplicate copies of all forms and keep a set in your office.

You should have all forms notarized. You can reduce the hassle of each family finding a notary by holding an information meeting for parents prior to a trip or event and inviting a notary to be present. Explain the activity or trip to the parents and students. Ask them to complete the forms before they leave the meeting and have them notarized on the spot. The meeting can fulfill the multiple purposes of information, registration, and presentation of requirements and rules.

Health forms can be filled out annually (or every six months) and kept on file for students who are active in multiple activities which require a health form. A parent's signature is required for each activity to confirm that the health information given previously is still current.

Most important, you must have immediate access to the forms when you need them. Work out a system that allows several people to know where the forms can be found. Keep the forms in a central location that can be easily accessed (not locked in a suitcase or the trunk of a car). If you are traveling in multiple vehicles, distribute the forms for the appropriate students/adults with a leader in each vehicle. Then if you are separated and in an accident, you will have all the appropriate information with you.

Collect the forms after the trip and keep them on file. Consult with a local lawyer about how long you should keep them in your records.

Specific Activities Liability Release Form

While the medical information form can be stored on file and used as long as the medical information is current, the activities release form needs to be fresh and specific each time it is used. (See the sample form in the appendix.)

The activities release form should describe the specific event and dates for which permission to participate is being given. The parent or guardian is giving permission for the student to be involved.

As stated earlier, many youth workers may have been told that a release form is a worthless piece of paper. Its value and importance continues to be a source of debate. A signed release form does not protect a leader or group from being sued by a parent for negligence. In legal terms, no organization can "contract away" negligence. A signed release does prove that the parent or guardian gave permission for their son or daughter to attend the event or activity. The leader is still responsible to act reasonably to provide safety and protection.

An organization can protect itself by listing on its release form the specific activities in which students will participate while under the care and supervision of the youth group leader. One of the major causes for lawsuits involving youth programs is surprise. When parents have little or no knowledge of the activities in which their children will be participating, they will be understandably upset.

The solution is to provide more information to the parents prior to the trip or event. Explanation of the activity can be given verbally to the parents at a pre-event meeting, but that information should also be in writing and given to the parents. Listing a series of "risky" activities and asking parents to initial their approval of their son or daughter's participation makes a much improved consent form that gives parents prior knowledge.

Listing specific activities on the release form requires the leader to produce a fresh form for each event. Keeping the basic information on either a computer disk or in the form of paste up art can reduce the work when the specifics of an activity change.

For what events or activities is a release form needed? A lawyer will tell you to have the form completed as often as possible. The trick is to always have it when you have an accident or incident. Here's my recommendation:

- overnight trip—always
- day trip out of your area—always
- any activity out of the ordinary—always
- normal, regular activities—get one form signed; keep one on file and a copy with you.

Check with a lawyer to work out the wording for the forms he or she recommends. Keep the lines of communication open with the parents of the young people who are involved with your program. More contact and communication mean fewer problems and reduce the chance of legal action.

Your commitment to safety and protection will be tested when a student arrives at the departure point for an overnight trip without his release (or medical) form. It would be very foolish to allow that person to go on the trip, despite the pressure you will feel from yourself and the other students. Send a message to everyone in your group about keeping the standards. They will thank you several years later for standing strong. Better yet, at the parents information meeting, get the parents to sign the forms on the spot. Have an early deadline for the paperwork and for the money to be paid. Don't let everything wait until the last minute.

Protecting Yourself

Establish an Oversight Group. Whether your ministry is large or small, demand from your church or organization a group of designated people to whom you will be accountable. The group could be composed of four to ten people who have interest in the youth ministry. A mixture of people by age, background, and occupation will give you a balanced group. Be sure to include some parents.

Discuss your plans for the youth group with this oversight group. Ask them for their feedback and suggestions. They are not meant to determine the strategy or goals of the ministry; they are there to help you find common-sense solutions to the problems you face and to give you honest feedback. Make safety a regular item for discussion. Report to them any accidents or near-misses you experience and ask for their help as you plan future events.

If you discuss safety matters with this group and heed their advice, you will build a strong defense for the "reasonable and foreseeable" preparations you make to protect the youth attending your program. Meet at least quarterly. Keep notes of all the meetings and file them in a safe place. On some pressurized day in the future, you will be glad you have verification of your commitment to safety concerns.

Keep Written Records. It seems that all youth ministry leaders hate pencils and paper. Still, leaders need to get over their fears and laziness about keeping written records. Build files and notebooks on all relevant information concerning safety matters. Prepare a written report for any accident that happens in your ministry (see appendix for a sample form). In counseling matters, keep written records of your conversations with students. Such records will be invaluable if you are ever charged with pastoral or counseling malpractice. Note dates and times as well as any directions or counsel you gave to a young person. These files should be kept under lock and key and must remain confidential. Because many lawsuits take place several years after the incident occurred, you can't trust your memory to recall all the necessary facts. Written records are a must.

Remember Who Is Your Protection. It is important to remember that while we are called to cooperate and act responsibly in affairs governed by humans, we do answer to a higher court and judge. Everything we do and say related to safety concerns should be pleasing to God and bring glory and honor to the name of Jesus Christ.

CHAPTER FOUR
How Well Do You Know Your Staff?

I couldn't figure it out. Carolyn had been one of our strongest student leaders during her junior year in high school. During her senior year when my hopes and expectations were so high for a great ministry in her school, she practically dropped out of sight. She seldom came to the meetings. Whenever I saw her on the streets or called her on the phone, she always seemed uneasy. For years I struggled with guilt, thinking that we had burned her out the first couple years of high school and contributed to her spiritual crash by keeping her too busy and not feeding her spiritual life or meeting her needs.

Five years later one of Carolyn's high school friends sat in our living room talking about her new job and reminiscing about her days in the high school ministry. I raised my question about Carolyn's senior year disappearance. Her friend said that Carolyn had had a difficult year because of her agonizing decision to have an abortion. Abortion? I didn't even know she was pregnant. Who was the father? The name struck me like a knife—Tony.

Tony had been one of our volunteer leaders in the youth ministry during the time Carolyn was in school. He was single, mid 20s, eager to serve God, and always ready to discuss the Bible. His commitment to the ministry had declined during the year we lost Carolyn. Through it all he had talked a good game and kept me in the dark. That dirty rat! He used his position in the youth ministry to hurt a young woman who we were supposed to be teaching biblical morality. How could I have been so blind to what he was doing behind my back?

Sexual Misconduct of Staff

One big negative about being in youth ministry for over 20 years is seeing numerous friends, professional ministers, and volunteers violate the sacred trust relationship by drawing teenagers into romantic and sexual relationships. Some of these crimes have been obvious (almost predictable); others have been a complete surprise and a total shock—committed by people I never would have suspected. I have learned from experience how skillful a sex offender can be when he or she is hiding the truth.

Is this a safety issue? How can it not be when young people are emotionally scarred and physically violated? It certainly is a legal issue and the reason for a growing number of lawsuits against clergy and counselors. Some clergy are presently being charged and tried for incidents that happened many years ago.

Sports teams talk about getting everybody on the same page of the playbook. A successful team is built with people who are qualified to be there, possess a strong desire to reach a common goal, show a willingness to set aside personal desires for the goals of the team, display an openness to instruction by the coach, and have an intolerance for anything less than their best effort. Youth ministry requires a similar team attitude and commitment to shared goals. Sadly many youth ministries drop into losing patterns because guys like Tony betray the team goals in their selfish pursuit of personal drives and needs. Other examples abound:

• One married male youth leader had a real tight bond with all of his junior high boys. He did so many special activities with these boys that the people of the church honored him repeatedly. He was very protective of his group and took a strong stand against cooperative events with other youth groups for theological reasons. A year later the church learned the shocking truth. This model youth leader had numerous homosexual encounters and relationships with the boys in his junior high group.

• A talented married male youth leader started home Bible studies with a 16-year-old girl and her friends (all girls) in her home after school. Within a few weeks interest in Bible study waned, but he continued meeting alone with the girl. The Bible studies included back rub massages which led to him fondling her regularly. He knew it was wrong and a betrayal of his commitment to his wife, but he couldn't stop. Neither could he tell any of his friends in the ministry or his pastor. Eventually the pastor was told by the mother after the daughter confessed to her. When the youth leader was dismissed, the rumor mill worked overtime.

• When a 16-year-old girl was legally removed from her abusive home, a female youth ministry volunteer (single, early 30s) offered to take her into her apartment. At the youth group meetings they seemed like a perfect match, almost inseparable. Later in the year their participation in the youth ministry declined to sporadic at best. The female volunteer said she was meeting the young girl's spiritual and emotional needs in a personal one-to-one relationship and didn't need to be at the group meetings. Within several weeks, the teenage girl told several of her friends that the volunteer had helped her realize she was a lesbian and that they were sharing that relationship together.

• A dynamic male youth leader developed a bad habit of focusing on several key students (usually girls) when he was on

CRY RAPE

"He tried to rape me in the car on the way here," Denise shouted as she entered the living room. She pointed her finger at Gary, one of our best volunteers. His face turned an ashen white.

"He did not!" countered Jennifer, who was 10 steps behind Denise, "I was in the back seat the whole time. He didn't do nothing." The color came back into Gary's face. Everybody laughed. Denise had made her first joke of the night.

But what would have happened if Jennifer hadn't been in the back seat? Denise was the kind of girl who loved attention and regularly bent the truth to serve her own purposes. Accused without a witness, Gary might not have stood a chance.

We wised up! None of our male staff drove any females alone to any of our meetings the rest of the year.

ministry trips without his wife. He would shower these special girls with extra attention and win their loyalty with long, deep discussions about the hurts of life. The young teenage girls loved to sit next to him and lean their head on his shoulder while he talked about God's love. He knew one particular girl was especially open to his leadership because of the recent disappointments in her life. She was eager for a major change in her life, hoping his faith would rub off on her. Late one night after a long one-to-one talk, he attempted to take the relationship to a deeper level by leaning over to kiss her on the lips. When she rejected his advances, he explained away the whole incident as a big misunderstanding. When the young woman told a counselor six months later it set off an investigation process that cost the youth leader his position in the ministry.

The level of sexual contact and criminality in each of these cases including Tony's is quite different, but betrayal of trust is the common factor. Each of these ministry leaders and volunteers crossed the line of moral and ethical behavior which parents expect when they put their children under the supervision and influence of a youth ministry. These adults willfully used their positions of influence to gain some emotional or physical satisfaction from a young man or woman entrusted to their care. They exposed the vulnerability of each boy or girl, took advantage of it for their selfish reasons, and broke the trust.

When Staff Betray the Trust

The Kids Are the Victims. Physically,

COMMON MISTAKES IN VOLUNTEER RECRUITMENT

1. We avoid recruiting mature volunteers. We overlook people who have years of experience because we think a volunteer has to be young to relate to teenagers.

2. We sign up and employ volunteers too quickly without thorough screening and orientation.

3. We are overloaded with young, single college guys who have a natural sexual attraction with the younger girls in the group. Most guys mean well but aren't trained by leaders to understand the forces at work or the temptations they will face.

4. We recruit too few women and put them in non-leadership positions. Women tend to be more safety conscious than men and have plenty to offer when events and activities are being planned.

they may be forced into dealing with pregnancy, abortion, and sexually transmitted diseases. Emotionally, they will be scarred by the seduction and betrayal. They are eventually dropped from their "special status" with the adult leader. They feel the ridicule of their peers. Sometimes they are blamed for the dismissal of a popular youth leader. They feel guilt and shame for what they have done and the lies they have been forced to live. Their family relationships become increasingly tense. Spiritually, they lose faith in God and in Christian leaders. They see hypocrisy everywhere and resist trusting any spiritual counselor. Guilt, shame, and depression block their ability to pray. They often launch out on a self destructive lifestyle, believing nothing in life really matters. It's crash and burn for them.

Lawsuits and/or Criminal Prosecution Will Follow. None of the stories told at the start of this chapter provoked a lawsuit or criminal action. They actually happened (names and some circumstances were changed to protect the victims) several years ago when families were less prone to sue or expose such private matters to the public eye. Today many of the taboos about legal action have been removed. Even so, parents are still reluctant to put their teenager through a public proceeding that would attract media attention. However, there is a dramatic increase of young adults coming forward bringing allegations of being molested or abused when they were underage. Adult leaders who get sexually involved with children or teenagers can expect to be looking over their shoulder for many years waiting for the anger to be released in some type of legal action. The church or youth organization can also expect to be charged with some type of negligence for allowing an employee or volunteer worker to harm their child.

The Bad News Spreads. Parents, the media, the community, and students hear the news and judge the ministry accordingly. Bad news travels like wildfire, even when it isn't true. Good news seems to move like a snail. The sins of one person can bring down the good reputation of a whole church or youth organization.

The Youth Ministry Atmosphere Changes. Staff and students feel betrayed by the offender. The hypocrisy present in the offender makes everyone much more skeptical of each other, their faith, and their involvement in the youth ministry. Relationships are strained as people wonder what other secrets in the group have been hidden. There is a sense of shock and grief similar to a physical death. Students and adults go through the steps of grief (emotional shock, denial, anger, remorse, grief, and reconciliation) as the news of a leader's misconduct becomes public. Group members find it harder to trust each other because an important link of trust has been betrayed. Drops in enthusiasm and attendance are also common byproducts of a leader's misconduct.

Other Kinds of Misconduct

Not every misconduct situation revolves around sex. The sex issue is major because of the powerful dynamic forces involved. The appetites and attractions are strong; the consequences are equally rugged. It has been a fatal attraction in many great men and women for thousands (yes, thousands!) of years. Satan has gained a foothold in many people by following the path of money, sex, and power. Misconduct can also happen when staff are not properly screened or trained.

Ted came on the retreat as a last minute replacement to serve as a counselor. Several of the staff leaders knew him as a 27-year-old, mild-mannered, solid Christian man. He was assigned to a cabin with eight junior high boys who had come from difficult family situations.

At 2 A.M. the light was still on in Ted's cabin. The youth group supervisor decided the unusual amount of noise coming from that cabin was a good reason to stick his head in the door for a quick check. When he opened the door he saw Ted looking like a raging bull holding a 12-year-old young man in a vicious head lock. The emotional stress of putting eight young teens to bed had snapped Ted's patience. He was on the verge of doing something to this boy he would regret the rest of his life.

The youth group supervisor defused the situation and immediately moved another experienced counselor into the cabin with Ted for the night. When the leader debriefed with Ted, he realized that under his mild-mannered veneer was an angry man who snapped under pressure. In the rush to get enough counselors for the weekend, they had screened Ted in 10 minutes only three days before they left.

Staff misconduct can also include money mismanagement, drug use, alcohol, foul and abusive language, lying, racial prejudice, gossip, disrespect for authority, and any other sins listed in the Scripture. Of course don't forget the "sin" of disregarding the health and safety of the students in the youth program.

Everyone in the youth ministry will fall short of perfection, but the standards of attitude and behavior need to be set high because of the important task given to the staff. An effective youth ministry has a shared commitment to excellence and holiness that models to watching teens the Christian life. Everyone who joins the team needs to qualify in the necessary skills and lifestyle.

Staff Selection and Supervision

If a staff leader's mistakes can cause so much damage and hurt to people, it's just common sense to go to great lengths to select the right staff and eliminate the potential violators.

During the last 10 years the number of civil suit awards related to employee misconduct has increased 3,000 percent. The amount of money awarded in those lawsuits has increased 5,000 percent. More important than the money and the legal problems is the damage that has been done to young people. In light of what is at stake, every youth ministry should reexamine their process of accepting and employing leaders (both paid and volunteer) to be sure reasonable precautions are taken to screen out potential offenders.

No process is fool proof. The law wants to know if an organization has taken reasonable and consistent steps to obtain information that will help predict any potential dangerous behavior by an employee (volunteers too). How much information should an organization gather about an applicant? Lawyers argue the right of an organization to know versus the individual's right of personal privacy.

Reasonable action means following any leads or concerns a person's initial application might generate. If an applicant says he has been convicted of a criminal offense, the reasonable action is to find out the details of that situation. If he says he has not been convicted of a criminal offense and there is no other contradicting evidence to raise suspicion, the process should not go any further. Any prediction of an employee's behavior can only be made according to his past performance.

Consistent action means that a standard investigation for each level of leadership involvement has been established. That standard should be applied equally without discrimination to everyone seeking involvement in the ministry.

Screening Potential Staff (Paid and Volunteer)

I recommend the following steps in recruiting a youth ministry staff.

1. A Written Application. I will limit comments about the contents of an application to safety related matters. The application can also request all types of information concerning a wide area of topics such as interests, spiritual experiences, and beliefs.

Regarding safety matters, the application should ask about a person's education and employment records and phone numbers to confirm such records. Call these contacts and ask questions that will give you insight into the person's personality and behavior patterns. Experienced background investigators suggest you try to get past the personnel office and connect with a specific supervisor or teacher. They are often more open to give details that will be helpful to you. Any gaps in employment or education is cause for asking additional questions about the period of time in question. Confirm the information on the application to assess its truthfulness. On the application include these questions:

- Have you been convicted of a criminal offense? If yes, please explain. Will you give us permission to check your criminal record?
- Have you been convicted of child abuse or sexual abuse or been involved in any activity related to molesting or abusing youth? If yes, please explain. Can we check your record?
- What moving violations are on your driving record? Please list and explain. Can we check your record?
- Provide any additional questions about their background (drug use, affiliation with questionable groups, etc.)

Conclude the application with a statement for the person to sign and date: "I testify that my answers to the above questions are complete and truthful."

This information protects your youth ministry from charges that you knowingly involved someone with a record of negative behavior. Obviously the applicant can lie. But if you had no reason to suspect the applicant was lying, it will be difficult for a jury to hold you responsible for involving the person in your program. If you suspect that the information is not truthful for any good reason, you are responsible to probe deeper (as a reasonable person would) until you are satisfied you know the truth.

The process of checking records varies from state to state. In some states it is difficult and expensive to check criminal records. Most of the applicants you encounter will not likely have criminal records, but when you do find something, the content is usually significant.

Checking sex abusers and child abusers is regulated by state government. In many states you can obtain a request form for information on a person by calling the Protective Services (or Child Protective Services) in your state government. Filing the request form with name and social security and submitting a fee ($10–$20) will produce information on a person's child or sexual abuse record. Other states (New York is one example) have tougher restrictions on gaining information. Although legislation is pending to open this information, it is restricted at present and can only be obtained through criminal records. Check your state regulations. The FBI does have a national listing of known pedophiles. Call your local FBI office for information on how you could check your applicants against that list.

Driving records are easiest to obtain and probably are the most relevant to the type of staff we recruit into the youth ministry. You can easily make a case for the connection between the way a person handles a motorized vehicle and his or her projected performance on a youth ministry team. It certainly is relevant if you will expect them to drive youth as part of their job in the ministry.

It is not necessary to check all records (especially criminal) just because you asked for their permission to do so. Just asking can cause people to be more honest in completing their answers. Some people will withdraw themselves from the application process when you ask for permission to check. You don't need to know the details or pursue it any further. You have your answer—they don't belong on the youth ministry team. If you do check records, your policy and practice must be consistently applied to every applicant. You could be charged with a discrimination suit if you treat any one applicant different from another applicant.

2. Ask for References. Five references are adequate to get a picture of the applicant—relative who lives closest to the person (not a spouse or a child), employer, friend, co-worker, and pastor.

Design the reference form to meet your specific ministry situation. It helps the person writing the reference to know what job their friend is applying for. Give a brief description of your ministry. Ask questions which will give you insight into the applicant's maturity and character. Ask the hard questions directly and without embarrassment. Give them opportunity to talk with you directly about something they might feel uncomfortable writing. If after reading a reference you have questions, take the initiative to call the person for clarification or additional information. A sample reference form is listed in the appendix to illustrate how it can be done. Don't shortcut the reference process. There may be information from a reference source you can't get from anyone else and could be key to really knowing the applicant.

3. Interview. Ideally it is best to have two people interview an applicant. At least one interview should be done by someone in the leadership of the church or youth ministry who does not know the applicant very well. Interviewing someone you know well seldom turns up any new information. With all applicants, conduct a standard interview, asking each person a set of predetermined questions.

Find a professional who interviews job applicants and work with this person to determine the information you want to gain from your interviews. Develop questions that will uncover that information. You will want to know the applicants' expectations and reasons for being involved, their attitude toward teenagers, their relational skills, their ability to handle conflict and crisis, their special abilities, their legal or criminal history, and their spiritual commitment to Christ. Take notes during the meeting and fill them in more completely after the interview.

4. Final Decision. Work with a team of people (leaders in your church or organization) to make a determination on the applicants. It's more objective when one person handles the written information (application and references) and another person conducts the interview. Neither person should know the applicant well. Include in the final decision a member of the leadership team who does know the applicant well. Let the three people discuss the person from their particular perspective.

From a safety standpoint, the qualifications to be a youth ministry team member should include:
- responsibility
- decision-making ability

- good judgment
- trustworthiness

The consistency or inconsistencies of the person will become more readily apparent when discussed in a varied group. By using this information and taking time for prayer, the group can make a decision about the applicant's fitness for involvement on the youth ministry team.

It is worthwhile to consider having a professional investigative organization conduct the background checks of youth ministry staff. These organizations will check according to the specifications you request. If you are ever sued for having someone in your youth program who had a negative background, the agency would be responsible for whatever damages were awarded. The obligation would be theirs, not yours. They can conduct an investigation in a variety of areas, including credit, criminal, education, employment, driving, credentialing, and personal references.

No Shortcuts

This process is lengthy, but it protects you in several vital areas. It eliminates people who are only partially committed. You would have discovered this at some time during the first six months of their service. It gives you more confidence that the accepted applicant will not hurt the kids you care so much about. The person can still disappoint you, but you will know it was his or her doing, not your carelessness, that hurt the kids. This process will also serve you well if you are called to defend it in a legal proceeding. It will be clear that you took the precautions that a reasonable person would expect.

Volunteers are so hard to find that none of us want to place any hindrances in their way. At first glance this application system seems to be more a deterrent than incentive to volunteer recruitment. It makes the shortcut route look pretty good. I must confess that many times during my ministry in YFC, I have chosen the shortcut and placed people in the ministry who were safety risks to our most precious commodity—our young people. I have learned the hard way that poor decisions always come back to hurt you.

Having high standards for acceptance as a youth ministry team member can be a positive public relations spin for you. Parents and community people who hear about your stringent volunteer standards will view your youth ministry as responsible and trustworthy.

Training Your Ministry Staff

When an accident or an act of misconduct puts the spotlight of scrutiny on your ministry, investigators will check the appropriateness of the staff you have chosen to employ. They will also check the training you provided to your staff to prepare them to do their job. This section on training will again focus on the safety aspect of your curriculum.

Orientation Session. Volunteers need a two- to ten-hour basic training and orientation to the ministry. They need to know how the organization works and their role in it.

First Aid Training. A certain number of the staff need to complete the certified first aid training course. The remaining staff can take a simplified version of the first aid course to learn the basics. Enough staff should be certified that every event can have a trained, certified staff person in attendance.

Identifying Child and Sexual Abuse. All staff need a training class to learn to recognize the signs of abuse and how to report it within the organization so that a mandated reporter can inform the proper authorities. Instructors can be found at a local college or within a local child service or protection agency.

Suicide Prevention Training. Find a social worker who can help train you and your staff to respond to suicide threats made by teenagers.

Crisis Intervention Training. If the staff is building relationships with kids they will witness crisis. The important part of this training is how to recognize when they are in a situation where they are over their head and how to get professional help.

Pregnancy, Drug Abuse, and AIDS Training. These conditions touch more teenagers each year. Some volunteers can pursue additional training to specialize in these social problems.

Activity Training. This includes training to cover the specific activities and events held by the youth ministry (canoeing, biking, backpacking, etc.).

Maintain records of all your staff meetings and training sessions. Keep a folder on file for each staff member with their application, references, any notes from supervision meetings, and a record of the training they have completed.

Staff Behavior Standards

If we ask our staff to follow a high standard of behavior, we are responsible to provide them with clear and specific guidelines by which they will be judged. They should read and sign this document before they start working in the ministry. All staff should re-sign this sheet each year to remind them of their commitment. You can create a form that fits your situation. Here's a sample:

Staff Behavior Standards

Name of staff/volunteer:

Social Security #:

This staff behavior standards document is to be read and
    signed by all staff annually.

    1. Any verbal or nonverbal sexual behavior with any student is inappropriate.

    2. Dating or going out with any high school student is forbidden.

    3. Discretion must be used in dealing with all students, especially regarding physical contact. Innocent behavior can be misinterpreted. A hug around the shoulders is not sexual abuse, but a full body-to-body hug, stroking, massaging, or an affec-

tionate kiss raises questions. Any overt display of affection should be made in a public setting in front of other group members.

4. Sexual gestures or overtures to a staff member by a student should be reported to the youth leader so that discussion can be held with the student.

5. Buddy systems should be used by staff whenever possible, especially when working with students of the opposite sex.

6. One-to-one counseling with a student should always occur in a public place—never alone in a car or a private place.

7. Driving alone with a student of the opposite sex should be avoided at all times, especially when working with troubled teens.

8. If it is necessary to ride or drive alone with a teen, special care is to be taken with a student of the opposite sex.

- Don't sit close to one another in the car.
- No physical contact.
- Do not stop the car to talk.
- If you must stop, turn on the inside light of the car.
- Avoid physical contact when saying goodbye (hugs and kisses).
- Be aware of the time when you depart and arrive. Mark those times in your diary or record.

9. Romantic or sexual attraction for a student by an adult leader should be brought up and discussed with the ministry team leader for prayer and guidance.

10. All suspicions of child or sexual abuse must be reported to the ministry team leader who will report it to the mandated reporter in the organization. That person will call it in to the abuse hotline.

11. Any knowledge or suspicion of any youth ministry staff having an inappropriate relationship with a student must be reported promptly to the youth ministry leader. If the person in question is the leader the report should be made to the supervisor of that person.

Have you been involved romantically or sexually with any student in the youth ministry at any time during the past year?
_____ yes _____ no

Do you know of anyone on the youth ministry team who is romantically or sexually involved with any student in the youth ministry?
_____ yes _____ no

Are you now a child abuser or have you ever been convicted of child abuse or sexual abuse?
_____ yes _____ no

If yes, please explain:

I certify that I have read the standards and agree to abide by them and that the statements above have been answered truthfully.

Signature _____ Date _____

Detecting Staff Misconduct

Innocent indiscretions are easy to spot and correct. Serious sexual misconduct violators are much better at disguising their actions and deflecting any inquiry into their behavior. They work hard to protect their secret.

Here are a few signs that signal possible trouble:

• A staff member spending time alone with the same person regularly.

• Physical contact (such as touching or hugging) more than normal.

• A teen becoming more and more dependent on one particular staff leader.

• A teen not mixing with other staff equally.

• Giving of unusual gifts between a staff member and a teen.

• How the two people in question look at each other.

• What the friends of the teen and the staff say or imply about their relationship.

• Reduced involvement of the staff member's spouse in youth ministry.

- A teen reducing involvement in regular youth programs but still showing up before and after activities to see a particular staff member.
- A staff member consistently giving rides to the same teen and resisting the offer of another staff member to do so.
- A staff member going to date-type places with a student outside of youth activities.
- A staff member treating one particular teen to food, tickets, and so on.
- A teen becoming extremely emotional without apparent cause.
- A defensive attitude or questioning of behavior standards by the staff member when the subject of possible misconduct is raised.
- A staff member's open defiance of a written standard of behavior and his or her minimizing of action when confronted.
- Other actions you would describe as inappropriate.

None of these signs should be taken alone as proof of staff-teen misconduct. These are only signals of what could be going on outside the youth ministry setting. The more signs present, the stronger your suspicions should be.

Staff need regular supervision to help them do their job in the youth ministry. Utilize a balance of group meetings and individual appointments. Use this time to address any concerns you have about how the staff person is relating (positively or negatively) to any of the students. Don't be afraid to openly ask staff if they are having any attractions or feelings toward the students.

If they are determined to be secretive, they will be. You have given them opportunity to discuss what might eventually disqualify them from the ministry. If you suspect some possible indiscretions, change their job and responsibilities to distance them from the teen in question.

If the evidence seems to prove misconduct, but the person will not acknowledge it, warn of your concern and promise the individual that he or she will be watched closely. You are expecting that person to live up to the standards of behavior that he or she signed. Remind him or her of the damage this relationship will have on the teen and request that he or she stop any inappropriate action for the sake of the teen. The person may become upset and quit the ministry, accusing you of a lack of trust. Such a reaction may provide the best solution to the problem, for they are probably covering up and deflecting the pressure back on to you. Also, have a staff member of the same gender talk to the teen in question cautiously and discreetly about how he or she would describe his or her relationship with the adult staff member. The young person's responses can provide additional, helpful information.

Take Action without Delay

Once you have conclusive evidence that the standards have been violated, take prompt action. Arrange a meeting with you and the governing board or supervisor over the youth ministry. Don't be afraid to dismiss or reassign the person to a ministry for a different age group. It will send a strong message to the rest of the youth ministry team that you are serious about the standards.

If you find that the person has been behaving immorally, you must alert the governing body of the organization and bring him or her under discipline. You need to carefully confront the student involved, using a same-gender staff member to find out what has happened.

At some point, the parents need to be told about what happened and what has been done to resolve the problem. This is always very messy and demands plenty of prayer. The senior leader of the church or organization needs to lead this process of confrontation, repentance, healing, and reconciliation.

If the teen-staff relationship has involved criminal activity, such as having sex with a minor, the parents must be informed immediately. If they choose to press criminal charges, the church or youth organization should recommend that each party obtain an attorney and conduct any communication through the attorneys. The organization must maintain a neutral stance and not appear to side with either the violator or the victim. The legal system will deal with the issue. Efforts can be made through the attorneys to deal with the relevant spiritual issues by involving a pastor at an appropriate time. If the news media becomes interested, appoint a single spokesperson through whom all communication is given. All other staff should be instructed to make no comment on the matter. The interests of the alleged victim and the accused are to be protected from any statements that might injure their reputation. The less said, the better.

Avoiding Future Problems

When Barry got caught messing around with a young girl in his youth group, nobody could believe it. His wife was so gorgeous. Why would a high school girl interest him? Though Barry had only been at the church for 15 months, the youth ministry was going better than anyone ever expected. As he was being dismissed, someone talked to his former employer at a church halfway across the country. The man from the former church admitted that Barry had been dismissed from their church for the same reason. When asked why they hadn't told the new church, they answered that they wanted to give Barry a fresh start without being hounded by a bad reputation. Besides, no one from the new church had asked.

Perpetrators of sexual misconduct often repeat their mistakes. Unless they have specific accountability to those who knows their flaws and are watching them in their new assignment, it is most likely that they will return to their old patterns. If someone is dismissed from your ministry, it is best for that person to stay out of ministry leadership for an extended period of time until a restoration process has been completed. If this person ignores your counsel and seeks a new assignment, take the initiative to make sure the new employer knows exactly who they are hiring. You won't be popular, but you will be protecting the safety of a young person in that youth program. Ask the potential new employer what specific precautions they are taking to guard against another violation. When you are hiring, be sure to ask all former employers and co-workers (reference checks) direct questions about any past sexual misconduct.

The possibility of misconduct should motivate you to screen and supervise diligently. Though it is time consuming, it is worth every effort to keep abuse out of your youth ministry. When a staff member betrays a young person's trust, it does enormous damage to people and the ministry while draining emotional energy and enthusiasm from the youth ministry team. Dealing with problems is even more time-consuming.

People make the difference. Two chapters of a youth organization can have the same operations manuals and resources and produce entirely different results. Any denominational church can have a good or bad reputation in a community depending on the quality of the leadership. Building a good youth ministry team and training them to work together is essential to a safe program.

ARE YOU A SEX ABUSER ... ?

Someone reading these words has a secret to hide. Right now or at some time in the past you have been involved in some kind of romantic or sexual relationship with a student in your youth ministry. If it's you—keep reading.

How long can you keep this secret? It's not a question of *if* you are discovered; it is only a matter of *when* everyone finds out. Perhaps you feel powerless to change or are just terrified of the consequences if you tell the truth. You keep hoping time will pass and all this will just go away.

You won't break the domination of this immoral relationship until you confess your situation to a trusted leader. It's the first step to breaking free. The consequences will be painful initially, but if you wait until you are exposed by another person the consequences will be much more severe. Your repentance and remorse will always be questioned because you didn't come forward. It will be hard for people to trust you again.

Don't keep this a secret. You will never feel any relief until you go with your trusted confessor to the person under who's authority you minister. Pray together and ask them to map out plans for you to repair the damage done to others and restore your integrity.

CHAPTER FIVE
Buses, Vans, and Automobiles

"I'm going to do it."

"You stay right where you are. I warn you—I will not stop this car."

Moments later the six students riding in the station wagon on the way to the youth retreat watched in disbelief as Jerry defied his youth leader and crawled slowly out of the rear passenger side window of the moving car. Jerry, 17, was known in the youth group for his radical stunts to get attention. The youth leader was tired of Jerry's immature attitude and was determined not to give in to his little self-promoting circus.

With the car continuing to roll down the interstate highway at 65 miles per hour, Jerry crawled onto the roof of the car and peeked into each window before exiting into the rear gate window of the station wagon. While the students in the car were giving Jerry the cheers he craved, the volunteer leaders driving behind the car had watched in shock the whole performance waiting for the worst to happen. Eyewitnesses said they saw Jerry lose his grip at least twice and could not explain how he had not been blown off the top of the car.

The volunteer drivers who had witnessed this stunt rushed to the youth leader when they arrived at their destination to express their anger and disbelief. The youth leader, who often worried about his reputation as fun loving, downplayed the

67

whole incident and said Jerry knew what he was doing. If he had fallen off it would have been his own fault. It would have served him right. As a youth leader he was tired of catering to Jerry and was determined not to delay the trip by stopping the car to deal with him.

True story! Here's another—

A youth leader tells of driving in a car caravan coming back from camp. The side door of a mini van opened while they were moving on the highway. The young man who had been sitting on the floor leaning against the unlocked door fell out onto the highway. Fortunately the pastor driving behind the mini van saw what happened and was able to stop in time to pick up the boy who escaped with only minor scrapes and bruises.

Sadly, a group in California didn't escape so easily.

A volunteer driving a pick up truck home from a youth event allowed 10 students to sit in the bed of the truck. During the trip he lost control of the truck. It rolled over several times. Miraculously no one was killed, but all the students were injured, some severely. The volunteer carried liability insurance for only $25,000 per person and $50,000 per incident. The group for whom he was driving took a major financial hit settling all the lawsuits. The pain from that tragic accident will continue to afflict the families of everyone involved for a long time.

Guilty! That's how most of us in youth ministry have to plead when charged with violations of safety involving buses, vans, and automobiles. These are three extreme examples of safety violations, but they reveal the danger involved when you mix young people, vehicles, and leaders who ignore safety issues.

Everybody has their own story. While interviewing youth workers for this book, the issues of vehicles and safety came up more often than any other subject. Most youth workers admit overloading vehicles with too many people, breaking the speed limit, not using seat belts and other offenses for which police routinely write tickets. Also on the mind of most youth workers are the qualifications of the people whom they call upon to drive for their events and the mechanical condition of most church-owned vehicles.

Transportation is the most easily recognized danger in youth ministry. Safety violations and shortcomings make the average church and youth ministry organization quite vulnerable to tragic accidents and subsequent charges of negligence.

Time to Get Organized

An increasing number of churches are recognizing the need for a transportation committee which sets a policy and monitors drivers and vehicles. The committee could consist of four to six people with representation from the pastoral staff, the trustees, parents of youth, and the youth ministry staff.

The transportation committee should meet frequently until they produce a written policy statement. Once they have established the ground rules of operating the vehicles under their care, their meetings could be conducted quarterly.

The written policy statement should address the usage of any church-owned vehicles (by who and for what), designation process of qualified drivers, responsibilities of the driver before, during, and after the trip, and written assignments for those responsible for maintenance and upkeep. A sample working policy can be found in the appendix.

An additional policy should be established for the youth ministry's use of "borrowed" vehicles owned and operated by parents and volunteers. Every potential driver should be subjected to a standard of qualifications so no student is ever placed with an unsafe driver.

Who Can Drive?

There are several key qualifications that drivers need to meet.

Acceptable Age: The person should be at least 21 years old, but check with your local insurance agent. Some companies require that drivers be 25.

Driving Record: Each driver's record should be checked for traffic violations and accident records. The committee should consult with its insurance company to decide what constitutes a satisfactory record.

Personal Insurance Coverage: The committee should know the amount of insurance each driver carries on their personal policy. It is wise to set a minimum level of coverage required to be a driver for the youth ministry.

Agreement to Safe Driving Standards: The committee should provide a written statement describing responsible driving. Each driver should read and sign the statement which is kept on file by the committee. Any driver reportedly violating the agreed standard must be confronted.

Helping Drivers Do their Best

Drivers are special volunteers who deserve quality treatment. Volunteer drivers need the careful support of the youth ministry leader so that they can do their best job.

Written Directions and Information. Every driver needs written directions to the destination (including a map segment and phone number). Provide in the same packet any money needed for gas or tolls and any special instructions about the trip (i.e., planned stops to eat and use the restrooms).

Adult Support. Depending on the length of the trip, the driver needs another capable adult driver traveling with him or her. Assistance is needed to share driving, handle directions, and deal with any distractions in the vehicle. Requiring leaders to drive home after tiring weekends with little sleep puts the youth in that vehicle at risk. A reasonable alternative is to bring on the trip qualified adults whose main responsibilities are to drive, serve as support staff, and stay well rested for the trip home. The extra drivers are also insurance in case any leader is injured or becomes ill and is unable to drive home.

Trial Run. Make sure every driver has a practice run in the vehicle they will drive prior to the trip. Driving a van or pulling a trailer is a different experience than driving a passenger car. Give adequate opportunity to practice tight turns, parking, braking, and backing up until they feel comfortable. Give attention to the seat position, checking for any changes needed to operate the accelerator and brake pedals and use the mirrors. Your drivers need to feel comfortable and confident to do their best job for your youth program.

Emergency Plan. Prior to the trip, discuss with all drivers your instructions for communicating with other drivers and handling emergencies. If you are traveling caravan style and someone needs to stop immediately or at the next rest area, what will your signal be? What should a driver do if they are separated from the caravan? How will you handle bad weather or driving conditions? After discussing the possible difficulties, the leader and the drivers can spend some time together in prayer asking God to help them as they serve.

Follow the Example. The head of staff sets the pace. The volunteer drivers need to see the one who makes the rules living by the same rules. Uniform observance of speed limits, seat belt requirements, and other guidelines is a practical demonstration of unity by the leaders before the students.

Student Drivers

Try to find an insurance agent who would approve high school students driving for youth group activities. They don't exist. Take the hint. We are foolishly putting ourselves and our youth at great risk when we let a teenager drive.

Most of us have felt the pressure of a teen who wants to drive for us. They play on our emotions (don't we trust them?) and offer to solve our immediate problems (we didn't plan for enough drivers). It is tempting. Having a clearly written policy about qualified drivers takes the pressure off of us. We are protected by the written rules of our church or organization.

How do you handle the student who is insistent on driving? You can't stop him from driving to your events or meetings. You should discuss his request to drive with his parent(s). If they approve, instruct him to meet you at your destination, not at your departure point. No students under your supervision should ride with the teen driver at any time. If he or she is driving friends to the meetings take the initiative and talk to all the parents involved, informing them of your policy and their responsibility if they permit their teens to ride with the young driver.

Vehicle Safety

Equally important with qualified drivers in the quest for safe transportation are reliable vehicles. Failure to provide or maintain quality vehicles for transporting students can be the primary reason for a tragic accident and the basis of a liability judgment against your youth ministry.

A youth pastor in New York State is thankful his church started using the youth ministry vans during the day to help with the nursery and day care school. The state requires a mandatory vehicle inspection every six months for vans used in nursery school operations. The youth group benefits because now problems and dangerous situations are fixed immediately. The vans have never been in better shape.

Don't wait for your state to enact similar strict inspection regulations. For the safety of the students you love, voluntarily submit to a qualified vehicle inspection every six months. Keep good records. It will protect you from accusations of negligence. You will also be alerted to problems with brakes, exhaust system, cooling system, as well as other maintenance needs before you are hundreds of miles away from home facing an emergency.

Before any trip (within 24 hours of departure) every vehicle should go through a "preflight" check.

You don't have to be a mechanic to check if you have:

- current registration and inspection stickers
- registration/insurance paperwork required to be carried
- an extra set of keys
- a flashlight
- a first aid kit
- a repair/supply kit (extra oil, wiper fluid, water, basic tools, garbage bags, rags, jumper cables)

- tools to change a tire and an inflated spare tire.
- seat belts in working order
- functioning lights and signals
- wiper blades in good condition
- snow brush or ice scraper for winter conditions.

Looking under the hood:

- Are belts tight? Any frayed or brittle? It's always smart to carry an extra set. You always seem to need them when auto parts stores are closed.
- Check the oil, transmission, radiator, and brake fluid levels.
- Battery terminals clean? Wires in good shape?
- Hoses in and out of radiator in good shape?
- Is the air conditioning unit functioning properly?
- Check tires for proper inflation and any gashes or bubbles.
- If pulling a trailer, check lights and tire inflation.

A member of the transportation committee who is solid in basic mechanics can play a key role helping you inspect each vehicle before each trip. It can be a special ministry for someone to see you off before each trip with a vehicle check. It will take pressure off the leader's mind to know that each vehicle has been "cleared for takeoff." Prepare a checklist which can be used for each vehicle. The "inspector" can keep a written record of the precautions you have taken to provide safe transportation.

Protecting the Ministry-Owned Vehicle

While every volunteer vehicle should be treated with the highest care, the vehicles owned by the church or youth ministry require some special stewardship. When a vehicle is driven by multiple drivers, accurate records are a must. It is simple to produce a short sign-out form to be completed each time the vehicle is used (see sample in the appendix).

When returning the vehicle, the driver should make note of any problems or trouble he or she had while using the van. Immediate attention can be given to reports of noises in the engine or of body damage. Requiring vehicles to be cleaned inside and outside when they are returned lengthens their life of service to the ministry. People treat clean vehicles with more care and caution. A dirty, cluttered vehicle triggers an attitude of thoughtless abuse by students and adults.

Everyone signing out the vehicle and driving it on youth ministry activities should read your basic rules of the road and sign their name acknowledging their acceptance of those standards.

Basic Safety Standards

The vehicle should not be overloaded. Have a legal limit clearly marked on the sign-out sheet.

• Every person should have a seat and should use a seat belt when the van is in motion. No sitting on the floor or on the laps of other people. (Some people may feel that using seat belts at all times is annoying, but it is a smart and necessary requirement.)

• No doors are to be opened when the vehicle is moving. All doors should be locked. No body parts should be protruding out of the windows.

• No students are to leave the vehicle while on the roadway stopped in traffic or at a traffic signal ("Chinese fire drills" or similar stunts are forbidden).

• No passenger should hinder or distract physically the driver of the vehicle while it is in motion.

• When the vehicle stops, no passenger should exit until either the engine is turned off or the driver gives specific verbal permission.

• Nothing is to be thrown out of the vehicle.

Insurance

Liability insurance is a top concern for any vehicle owned or used by your youth ministry. There is a simple answer to the question of how much insurance you should carry: you can't carry too much. Obviously it pays for insurance agents to give such advice, but the increase in costly lawsuits should motivate every youth leader to reexamine his or her coverage.

No one should drive for the youth ministry activities with minimal amounts of liability insurance. In most states, each volunteer should carry at least $100,000/$300,000 liability coverage ($100,000 maximum per person and $300,000 maximum per incident) plus a $1 million personal liability umbrella policy. (Chapter 3 contains additional information about insurance.)

Vehicles (especially vans and buses) owned by the church or youth organization require greater liability coverage than $1 million. In the event of a tragic accident with a van or bus involving serious injuries and fatalities, $1 million of coverage will be exhausted quickly. Inadequate insurance coverage can seriously damage the assets of individual volunteers and organizations who will be targeted by the lawsuits. The tragedy of the accident will be enough trauma without being compounded by financial struggles.

Handling a Breakdown

Breakdowns are a gift from God! Young people learn more about the Christian faith of their leader when the van breaks down on the trip home than they did during all the programs and meetings of the retreat. For every good message we deliver to young people, God gives us opportunities to live out our faith when we are tempted to lose our temper, worry, or curse the lousy bus or van. It's a lesson in real life they will never forget.

So after you have thanked God for such a great opportunity to demonstrate the Christian faith, you have to deal with this major inconvenience. It can be anything from a flat tire to some type of engine trouble. Here is a plan of action:

1. Do your best to park the vehicle in the safest spot you can find away from the flow of traffic. You may be sitting there for a while, so make it the best possible spot you can safely reach.

2. Unless you are faced with some imminent danger such as a fire in the engine or exhaust fumes, keep the students in the vehicle. Be firm. You don't need additional supervision responsibilities at that time.

3. Look for the problem and decide how serious it is. You

may want an additional knowledgeable person riding with you to help you. In addition, try to determine where you are stopped so that if you call for help you can give your location accurately.

4. Discuss together what kind of help you need and think about where you could obtain it. Remain calm and confident that God will help you through this difficult moment.

THE SPECIAL CHALLENGES OF WINTER DRIVING

Mention winter driving, and everyone thinks of slippery, icy roads. When the ice melts, the conditions can be just as hazardous if you aren't prepared. Don't forget to bring:

1) Extra windshield wiper fluid—it will go faster than ever when the snow is melting and the road is wet.
2) Rags or towels to wipe down the headlights. A day of driving in the slush puts a heavy film on the headlights, reducing the power of your beams.
3) Sunglasses—the sun hitting the snow can be blinding.

5. Return to the vehicle and talk with the students. Tell them openly and honestly the situation. Pray together for God's protection and help. Ask them for their best cooperation and support. It may mean remaining in the vehicle while you try to obtain help or perhaps vacating the vehicle while you jack it up to change a tire. If they leave the vehicle, they should move together to a safe place that you designate and stay there. Most important, keep them away from the road.

6. Exercise your best option. This is a time when a cellular phone (borrowed from a friend or church member just for emergency use on this trip) or having a CB radio becomes a useful tool. You can also solicit passing cars for anyone with a car phone. With the phone, you can call the police or any type of road repair and assistance.

Here is where thoughtful preparation pays dividends. The youth leader needs to carry either a road assistance/towing service membership card or a major credit card provided by the church for emergency use. It is also wise to have a transportation committee member on call at home during this travel time. The member can be praying for you during travel time and also be ready to receive any calls for assistance or advice. The member may want to discuss any repairs that need to be made or dispatch a backup vehicle to come and pick up the stranded passengers. That committee member can also activate a phone chain to alert parents to the probable late return. Planning can provide a helpful voice at the other end of the line who can help share the pressure.

Caravaning

This almost universal method of transporting a youth group to a weekend retreat can be a nightmare if you don't prepare all the drivers to follow a few basic rules.

- Every driver needs specific written directions. Each driver should be able to tell his passengers when you'll make the food and restroom stops.
- Agree on a distress signal (flashing headlights twice, for instance) that tells the lead vehicle to stop.
- Talk through what a driver should do if the vehicle becomes separated from the group.
- The driver of the lead vehicle should be thoughtful of the whole caravan when changing lanes, making turns, and going through traffic lights. All cars should use turn signals to alert the caravan to turns and lane changes. Avoid changing lanes excessively.
- No competition or socializing between cars.

Dangerous Situations

Fogged or Iced Windows. Drivers should never drive their vehicles when the visibility is poor. Keep the front and back windows clear. Drivers cannot make good decisions if they cannot see the traffic coming from all directions. Don't be lazy. Keep the windows clear.

Backing Up. Fogged windows and impaired vision can make backing out of a parking space dangerous. If you are not sure what is behind your vehicle, put it in park and get out to take a look. If you are in a tight squeeze, have a responsible student guide you out.

Braking Time and Distance. Take time to get adjusted to the brakes of a different vehicle you have been asked to drive.

Remember that a loaded vehicle takes longer to stop than an empty one. Don't tailgate other vehicles—allow plenty of space.

Bad Weather Conditions. Slow down! Most accidents are caused by excessive speed for the prevailing road conditions.

Fatigue. Driving through the night with one driver is foolish and dangerous. Provide relief. Make sure your drivers get some sleep before the trip home. Better yet, have designated drivers who do not wear themselves out participating with the students during the trip.

Hiring a Professional Bus

Sometimes it is a better choice to leave the driving to someone else. You can take pressure off your staff and keep them focused on the students and the program by removing them from the responsibilities of transportation.

Don't be shy about checking the safety records and reputation of professional bus companies. Ask the bus company for names of other groups they have serviced. Call those groups for a recommendation.

There are several safety concerns particularly related to using a professional bus company. Your group should appoint one staff leader as bus captain to serve as liaison with the driver. The bus captain represents your group and is the communication link with the professional driver throughout the trip.

Ask the professional driver about any safety concerns he or she wants enforced during the trip. Most likely the driver will ask people to remain in their seats while the bus is moving. No one should be sleeping in the overhead storage area or on the floor.

When the bus stops at a rest area, speak to all the students before they exit the bus. Set a time to be back on the bus. Warn students about traffic in the parking lot. Caution them about crossing the road to visit another restaurant or store especially if it is night time. Be sure to count and confirm everyone's presence before giving the driver permission to leave.

Professional bus drivers are known for their driving skills

and savvy. Unfortunately many of them also drive at high rates of speed consistently above the legal limit. If you feel uncomfortable about the speed or any aspect of the driving, do not hesitate to discuss it with the driver. Express yourself respectfully but be firm about your safety concerns. You are the customer, so the bus driver and his company should be trying to please you. Even if your concerns are not warmly received, the driver may be more conscious of safety during the rest of the trip because you spoke out.

If someone becomes ill on the bus, it is important to communicate immediately with the driver. He can use his radio to contact police or an ambulance if needed. The leaders should have the first aid kit available in the bus along with garbage bags, air freshener, and paper towels to clean up any mess. The permission/medical forms should be readily available to the leader, not packed away in storage under the bus.

When the bus drops your group at your destination, it may be wise to rent a car for the length of your stay. You may need a vehicle during your stay at a camp or resort to carry any student who might need medical attention.

CHAPTER SIX
Camps and Retreats

"I'll never forget my first day of eighth grade church camp. Mark, George, and I were the three musketeers primed and ready to run wild and meet girls. By the end of that first day the three of us had spent most of our time focused on the same female.

"She was older and more mature than the other girls at camp. Mark met her during the softball game when a bat thrown 30 feet straight up came down squarely on the top of his head. George met her 30 minutes later shortly after he crashed into the backstop chasing my errant throw from left field.

"Not to be outdone by my buddies, I met her that evening. I walked out of her cottage with a huge red mark on my neck. It wasn't from passion. I had been running through the darkness between the buildings chasing girls when I was clotheslined by a metal stabilizing wire attached to a light pole. Our special lady took good care of us that first day, but we all agreed that the camp nurse was a little too wrinkled for our eighth-grade tastes."

Crazy things always seemed to happen at camp. It was never like being home. New setting. New people. No parents. The counselors were young, fun-loving, and sometimes wilder than the kids.

Thirteen years later eighth graders were chasing me through the darkness of an upstate New York camp. I had a piece of adhesive tape on my forehead, and they were determined to take it off. Our nighttime "wear 'em out" game was a creative adaptation of cops and robbers. The tape on my forehead meant I was still alive. When it was ripped off I was "dead."

Apparently my number was up. Three husky guys wrestled me to the ground and began pawing at my face. It stopped being fun when their fingernails ripped across my nose and eyes. At that moment I realized there were 800 fingers pawing at 160 eyes all across that camp. I thought I had created a wild and crazy camp game designed to let my junior high kids do what they did best—chase each other and tussle with each other. Instead I might have been the architect of injury and eye damage for one or more of them.

The "camp attitude" had overridden my good sense. It's doubtful I would have run this cops-and-robbers game at a normal youth group activity back home. I wanted my kids to be excited about being at camp. There shouldn't be anything wrong with wanting students to have great memories of camp. It just seems that the camp atmosphere causes the leader to loosen the safety standards when in fact the situation calls for them to be tightened and strengthened.

Think about it. Do we let our young people run unchecked in the dark through the hallways of our church building or outside church property at night? Yet many of us allow it when we are at a camp in an outdoor setting full of surprises and hazards.

Linda organized a late night hide-and-seek game for her youth group at last fall's retreat. During the game she got scared watching her crew run through the woods, jump off ledges, and crash into each other. One girl ran into a clothesline (sound familiar?) and ended up on the ground with the wind knocked out of her. Linda tried to calm their reckless approach to the game. Suddenly it wasn't as much fun.

The next morning at breakfast she saw one of her girls cradling her arm tenderly. An X-ray that afternoon showed a broken bone. She hadn't said anything last night because she didn't want to spoil all the fun. During the drive home, Linda mentally practiced how she was going to explain to the parents exactly what was going on when the accident occurred.

Camp is different. Things happen there that don't happen at home—adventure, romance, activities, spiritual openness, and accidents. The basic safety risk for camps and retreats is underestimating how different the camp setting is as a potential safety hazard. We walk into the facility with a relaxed attitude toward safety. Many professional camp directors believe the average youth leader doesn't understand that the normal safety policies from home aren't enough when you arrive at camp.

Ingredients for Safe Camps and Retreats

The Camp Director. Successful and safe camps start with a relationship—youth leader and camp director working together. Some camp directors are actively involved in every aspect of the camp while others serve only to provide basic maintenance for the buildings. Months in advance the youth leader needs to visit the camp and talk with the camp director to establish a working relationship.

We got off to a real bad start with a camp director in New England during a winter retreat. I found out months later that breakage and damage at the camp had occurred with all the other church groups in the weeks prior to our visit. During the first 30 minutes on the grounds, students broke a light and a chair. The camp director got real gruff with us. During supper, one of our staff flicked some chocolate pudding on a student at the table, setting off a minor pudding war. The camp director rushed out of the dishwashing room, grabbed the microphone, and chewed out all our students and staff. He sensed that we weren't going to control our students, so he stepped in to protect his property. I am embarrassed to confess that the rest of the weekend we allowed our staff to make fun of "Mr. Grumpy" in all the meetings and joked with the teenagers about trashing the camp.

Are youth leaders and camp directors partners or adversaries? Experienced camp directors feel pressure when they host youth leaders who are soft on safety issues. Their sense of responsibility compels them to step in and speak up before someone is injured. Ideally, they can use the moment to educate the group leaders to the risks and dangers they have learned from weekly experience, but they know they are taking the risk of becoming the bad guy. Misunderstanding and bad feelings can be avoided by pre-trip meetings in which activities and safety standards are discussed in detail.

Many camps offer the services of professional staff to supervise and lead the recreation, including lifeguards, water craft instructors, winter sports supervisors, and registered nurses. Camp directors often don't understand why many youth groups are reluctant to spend a little extra money to hire additional camp staff who could help monitor and supervise activities. For a nominal fee per weekend, experienced camp staff could be added to the team of workers serving and protecting the visiting group. Safe camps and retreats start with a partnership between host and visitor.

The Camp Facilities. Nothing beats seeing a camp firsthand and meeting with the director. In addition to eyeballing the camp grounds, inquire about the accreditation of the camp. The most reputable accreditation is with the American Camping Association (ACA). This secular organization has a strict set of safety standards for physical buildings, staffing, programs, and services. A camp accredited by the ACA demonstrates a high commitment to safety and excellence. A Christian camp can also be associated with Christian Camping International which also requires a high standard of excellence. Investigating a camp's accreditation and association membership gives a strong basis for judging its quality.

Primary safety issues to investigate include:

1. Check that the buildings and sleeping quarters are protected with working smoke detectors, recently serviced fire extinguishers, and emergency exits.

2. Walk through the camp observing electrical wiring, sani-

tary conditions, storage of hazardous materials, and the natural and man made hazards on the grounds.

3. Ask about the accident record at the camp during the past 12 months.

4. Inspect the sports equipment and facilities of the camp to determine how well they are maintained.

5. Learn of the accessibility of medical facilities and services.

6. Ask what professional staff are available to you through the camp (registered nurses, lifeguards, waterfront instructors, etc.).

7. What insurance coverage does the camp carry that would apply to you and your group?

The Food Service. Whether your group contracts to use the camp's food service or elects to provide their own cooks, special attention must be given to food preparation. An accident on the water front or the snow sledding hill is rare and usually affects only one person, but a lapse in safety standards in the kitchen could cause the whole group to suffer food poisoning. Ask:

- Does the cook have training and experience in food service for large groups?
- Are the utensils, equipment, serving dishes, and food contact areas clean and sanitized?
- Is a dishwasher available to wash at legal standards of 100°F and rinse at 180°F? Are all items allowed to air dry?
- Are perishable foods refrigerated at temperatures below 45°F when they are not being served?
- Are precautions taken to prevent salmonella poisoning? (Salmonella bacteria is present in some uncooked eggs and some raw poultry.)
- Are workers required to wash hands frequently?
- Is smoking prohibited in food preparation and service areas? Are sharp knives and slicing machines used only by adults?

Staff Training and Emergency Preparedness. Here's a pop quiz for you and your camp counselors: What is the first rule of emergency response? Do you know it? You can't prepare your leaders for every bad possibility, but they need to know the basics so they can respond to the unexpected.

It was a dark and stormy night. The camp counselors were jolted out of their sleep by a loud crash on the roof of their cabin. The girls in the cabin began screaming and crying. Wind and rain were pounding against the cabin. It was totally dark; apparently the electrical power had been knocked out. What should counselors do in such a situation?

The first rule of emergency response is to think before you act. The counselors quieted the girls and quickly did a role call to determine if anyone was injured. With everyone okay, they gathered all the girls together and calmed them. They took control of the group and their emotions.

Calmly they talked about what they should do. Because they were safe and not being threatened by any conditions, they decided to stay put until either help came or daylight allowed them to see and assess the situation. That was a life-saving decision because the electrical power lines had fallen on to the porch of their cabin. Anyone stepping out of the cabin in the dark would probably have been electrocuted.

When the storm hit, a camp staff member who was assigned to emergency response got up to make an inspection of the camp. He saw the electrical lines down on the cabin porch and returned to the camp's electrical box to shut down the power. He had never shut down the power for the camp in that manner, but there was an emergency response notebook available to him which described what he should do.

The cabin counselors' response was the product of "what if" training. They hadn't specifically discussed the possibility of a tree falling on the cabin, but they knew that they should think before they took any action. They made sure everyone was safe and then proceeded slowly and cautiously. Any panic causing someone to run out the front door would have brought tragedy.

"There is no substitute for a trained, mature staff," says Bob Kobielush, president of Christian Camping International. Weekend counselors from our local youth groups need basic "what if" training.

- Do they know where the emergency exits are located in case of a fire?
- Do they have the number of the police or ambulance crew?
- Can they find a telephone?
- Do they know to whom they should report any trouble? How can that person be reached?
- Where is a first aid kit?

Give counselors as much information and training as possible. Talk through a wide variety of possible emergencies until the basics of immediate response are ingrained in your leaders.

Byron Emmert, veteran youth worker from Minnesota, knows the value of having an emergency response team ready and available. Byron wanted to bring a diabetic young man from his YFC club to summer camp. The young man's mother initially was against the idea because of his diabetic condition, but two weeks prior to camp Byron convinced her to train him so he could administer the injections if necessary.

The first day of camp Byron completely forgot to ask the young man if he had taken his morning injection until bedtime, when the second injection was scheduled. The young man told Byron he had forgotten in the morning so he gave himself an injection at 4:30 P.M. before supper. He assured Byron everything would be all right.

In the middle of the night Byron woke to the sound of the young man struggling to breath. He jumped to his aid and found him having some type of seizure. The young man had turned blue.

Byron struggled to open the boy's mouth, ignoring the pain as the teeth bit down on his fingers. He pulled the tongue out of his throat and thrust the bill of a baseball cap into the mouth of the young man to act as a tongue depressor. Throughout these stressful minutes Byron roused the entire cabin of guys and gave directions to find the camp director and nurse.

Minutes later they burst through the door and took over the

rescue effort and stabilized the young man. Byron stepped aside with a huge feeling of relief. He took one look at the blood dripping from the deep bite on his fingers and immediately fainted. (At the time, Byron did not realize that he should not have placed anything in the young man's mouth, especially his fingers! A person suffering from a seizure should be placed on his side and kept calm and comfortable.)

Was it worth the effort to bring a diabetic student to camp? Byron thinks it was. However, next time he will post a reminder sign for himself and the young man so he doesn't get off his injection schedule. Staff need to monitor young people with similar health needs. The students shouldn't be trusted to remember. Byron now realizes that when he knew this young man was off schedule, he should have obtained help from the camp nurse before they went to sleep. Most of all, Byron was glad a professional nurse was available to help immediately. He might not have had much more time to save the boy's life.

All staff and leaders need an emergency procedure briefing prior to the camp or retreat. Rehearse the basic safety procedures and response. The leader can select possible events and quiz each staff on how to respond. Written instructions and information on securing medical help should be provided.

Dangerous Camp Games and Situations

Mud Sliding and Assorted Variations. A camp counselor told me last week how they rescued their week of rain at camp by having a mud sliding event. Evidently he and many others are still unaware that some of the most tragic accidents and subsequent lawsuits involve mud events.

In a well-publicized case several years ago, a youth organization created a mud sliding pit. A student ran, slid across the mud, and crashed head first into the hardened earth at the end of the pit. The impact broke his neck and paralyzed him. After that incident, most youth organizations banned mud activities. Many insurance companies handling camp and youth activities specifically exclude it from coverage.

The principles of safety involved here apply to other games: 1) Avoid games that might result in head first collisions with other people or natural objects—the risk of a broken neck and paralysis is enormous; 2) Avoid games that incite reckless or overaggressive behavior; and 3) Avoid games that are hard to supervise—if you can't stop an activity quickly, you don't have enough control.

Cage Ball (Earth Ball). This large inflatable canvas ball is used for pushball type games. Injuries are the result of students being hit full force by the ball. A dangerous way to start the game is to have students from each team run from their end line to the ball in the middle of the field. The first team to reach the ball propels it forward into the approaching opponent. The results could be shown on a pro football highlights film. The second student is often knocked off his or her feet by the oncoming ball. It makes great video but the risk to the person absorbing the blow is unacceptable. Ban the running start. Also, the six-foot ball is more dangerous than the four-foot ball.

Students are also hurt when the crowds surrounding the ball are pushing to move the ball. It's a reverse tug-a-war with the forces pushing toward each other instead of pulling away. Someone who falls can be trampled by the onrushing mob.

The greatest danger using the cage ball is having anyone crawl on top of the ball during the game. That person can easily fall head first to the ground and suffer head or neck injuries. A youth ministry volunteer was paralyzed by falling off a six foot cage ball. The ball was sitting on the side of the field after it had been used. The volunteer attempted to climb on top on the ball so that he could walk on top of the ball while rolling it down the field. He lost his balance and fell headfirst to the ground. His neck was broken instantly.

Use of the cage ball requires intensive supervision. Most accidents with sports equipment happen on the sideline away from the attention of the leaders. In this case the cage ball should have been guarded by a staff leader who had strict orders not to let anyone mess with it. It should be deflated immediately or put away under lock and key.

The cage balls can still be used under controlled circumstances: 1) No running starts; 2) Fewer people on a team so the ball keeps moving; 3) Don't inflate the ball fully to reduce the impact of the ball hitting a person; and 4) Don't tolerate anyone jumping or climbing on the ball.

Pile-On Games. At one of my very first youth retreats I remember 200 students packed in a long narrow meeting room. The leader wanted to mix up the crowd and get everyone excited. He drew an imaginary line in the middle of the room and said at the count of three everyone should change sides as fast as possible. Doesn't that sound like great fun? A minute later the middle of the room looked like a Dallas Cowboys goal line stand. It took 10 minutes to unpile everyone. The innocent victims were the small young girls and boys who were pushed and trampled by all the bigger guys coming from the sides of the room. Three kids went to the hospital for X-rays. Five or six more were panic-stricken because they had been unable to breathe at the bottom of the pile. What a great way to start a weekend retreat.

Sports Games. Most camp and retreat injuries are connected to playing some type of sports. Many are unavoidable (once you make the decision to include sports in your schedule) and are common injuries. The major risks involve injuries to the head, neck, and eyes. Insurance companies warn against any throwing or launching of dangerous objects toward another person. Oversized sling shots used to launch water balloons, paint balls, or flour balls are excluded from coverage because of the potential to injure a person's eyes.

Just Don't Do It:
- Don't play on any athletic field without first inspecting it for hazards and dangerous debris.
- Don't use games that encourage any throwing of objects toward another person's face.
- Don't mix big and small, weak and strong students in contact

sports. The little guys usually get crunched.
- Don't make everyone in your group play the sports game. The reluctant participant is often the first one injured.
- Don't incite or encourage aggressive or rough play.
- Don't let athletic equipment be used without supervision.
- Don't hesitate to step in and stop a situation that is getting too rowdy, rough, or uncontrolled.

I helped create a sports situation that almost turned into a real ugly scene. At a summer youth conference, groups were encouraged to enter athletic teams in various sports for competition during the week. The boys basketball division was really lopsided. Most teams were weak and unskilled. Two teams were loaded with varsity athletes.

Instead of running the tournament as usual, I joined other leaders in suggesting that the two top teams play their own best-of-five series for the championship. What seemed like a great idea on Monday had us practically calling the national guard on Friday. We encouraged the competition between these teams from two different cities and backgrounds. Every day the games got more intense. The level of the players was far above the skill of the referees to control the game and make the calls. When the final gun sounded in game five, people were ready to fight. It took a long time to cool the players down. We had encouraged too much competition and allowed it to get out of control.

Good supervision of sports activities means watching for the people who are growing angry and looking to get revenge for what has been done to them. Be assertive and pull that student out of the game until he or she cools down. The gung-ho kid who is going crazy swinging his pillow in the giant pillow fight needs to feel the hand of a staff member on his shoulder cautioning him to ease up or sit out.

Hide-and-Seek (and All Variations of Nighttime Madness)
The second major setting for injuries at camps and retreats (after sports) is the late night "run wild" games. A youth leader gathered his group for late night hide-and-seek. Among the

rules—don't climb any trees. Of course the youth leader himself climbed a tree to hide. He fell out of the tree breaking both arms (do you doubt there is a God?). The youth leader is now suing the church for damages. Young people love these games, but we have to think through the risks and design a safety system to keep them from hurting themselves.

Twist and Run. This favorite camp game (you know all the variations—put your forehead on a bat and spin around ten times and try to run back to your team) is a prime example of how to modify a game to be both fun and safe. We usually have belly laughs watching people try so hard to run straight and ending up on the ground. It always seemed like a relatively safe and harmless game to me. During the interviews for this book several youth leaders told me of injuries using this game. One girl fell as she was running back to her team. Her head found the only rock on the entire field. Several more were injured when they crashed into other runners. The chance of injury seems remote, but the family of the person who is hurt might not understand those odds.

Should I stop using this game now because I know of several injuries it has caused? I don't believe you have to zap these games because of a few injuries. They are still usable if we will take some extra precautions for safety. For the twist around game a creative solution is to assign staff to run along side the students and act as spotters ready to catch them or break their fall.

Double Dare. This popular television show has taken many of the traditional youth ministry game ideas and used them successfully. They major on relays and stunts with plenty of messy goop. Notice the goggles on the eyes, the helmets on the heads, the padding on the elbows and knees, and the spotters throughout the course. Youth ministry can still use field event games at camps and retreats if we are willing to go the extra mile to protect the participants.

Careful game management involves numerous trained staff in position as spotters. Give them a communication plan to signal any dangerous activities and the ability to stop play immediately. Equip the spotters with whistles and an emergency signal. When they sound the signal, a main safety supervisor blows a portable air horn. At the sound of the air horn everyone knows to stop and kneel down immediately. With proper preparation and controls, youth ministries can still use games and activities.

All sports equipment for games must be carefully supervised before and after its use. Staff leaders must be assigned to put away all equipment immediately after it is used. Require the use of appropriate safety gear. Jazz up the gear so that it will be fun to wear. Going the extra mile includes having trained medical personnel (paramedics) on site throughout the games and activities.

Youth For Christ and a group of churches in Florida sponsored a big day of field events. It almost became a tragedy during the first hour when a young man had a severe asthma attack. The staff admitted later they weren't sure of what to do to help that young man. It wasn't a problem because the YFC leader had secured two paramedics from a nearby Navy base to be at the event. They moved in with their equipment and restored the young man's breathing.

Whenever I walk into a camp director's office at the start of a weekend or a week, I look at the phone and pray I won't have to use it during my stay at the camp to call some mom or dad with bad news. With good safety preparation and enforcement, your camps and retreats can be positive lifetime memories for your students.

Hotels and Resorts

It's a growing trend for youth groups to attend large conferences held at hotels and special resort areas. The rustic, remote camp ground has been replaced by Marriott or Radisson. While there is room for debate about the merits of using a hotel over a camp, the hotel definitely raises some unique safety issues.

The Hotel Setting

Most hotels are multi-story buildings in highly populated areas. If the design of the hotel includes balconies and high overlooks you must prepare for some young person dangerously leaning over the railing or sitting on it like a bird on a perch. If the windows open, they will be tempted to hang out or throw objects to the ground. Strict warnings and attentive staff supervision is absolutely necessary.

Swimming pools, hot tubs, and saunas are an attractive part of the hotel experience. The swimming pools tend to be small and overcrowded during a youth conference. Is there a hotel employee or a qualified conference staff member serving as lifeguard and enforcing safety standards? Are students following the written safety rules posted near the sauna and hot tubs? Are the hot tubs being cleaned and maintained throughout the weekend? A build up of bacteria in the water can cause illness to all bathers. If a hotel is not usually busy on weekends, their normal maintenance schedule may not be adequate for your weekend invasion.

Although the rooming accommodations in a hotel are usually much nicer than a camp setting, the small rooms (usually four per room) and the locked doors present supervision problems. Students have much more privacy. It is harder for staff to just "walk in" and discover some inappropriate behavior. Guys and girls have much more opportunity for romantic rendezvous undetected by staff. Instruction and enforcement of rules prohibiting coed gatherings in bedrooms is absolutely necessary. Staff must be diligent about guy-girl encounters in the private rooms.

The privacy of the rooms and the access to public shopping areas also increases the possibility of contraband materials (alcohol, drugs, etc.) being present at the conference. Students who are looking for trouble have an uncanny knack of finding the wrong people. Rules need to be clear and tough. Staff must be polite but tenacious about such destructive substances.

A clear policy about leaving the hotel property must be communicated to all students and staff. No one should be walking or sightseeing alone. Staff supervisors should either be with every group of young people or should know where they will be and when they will return. The type of staff supervision needed may vary according to the setting or the reputation of the area, but staff need to know the rules and enforce them strictly.

Using a hotel or resort site moves the camp retreat from a remote, protected location into the mainstream of humanity. The normal operations of the hotel and the area will continue throughout your conference experience. The leader needs to prepare for possible intruders who could harm the young people.

Our group was staying at a hotel in Florida for a winter break conference. A 16-year-old girl asked to be excused from the evening general session meeting in the conference room to return to her room for some headache medicine. We granted permission and posted a staff to watch her walk across the courtyard to her room. When she arrived at her room she turned to see three men 25 to 30 years old following close behind her. They had just come from the hotel bar and were looking for some action. They tried to talk her into inviting them into her room. When she refused, one man grabbed her and pushed himself up against her. She screamed and the staff leader on watch outside the meeting room came running. The police were called. They escorted the men off the property and warned them not to return. The young woman felt fear and anxiety throughout the rest of the week.

At a winter conference in a downtown hotel a middle-aged man stepped on to the elevator filled with 14-year-old girls. As the elevator moved from floor to floor he tried to start conversations with some of the girls. They did their best to ignore him and exited at their floor. One girl was left in the elevator alone with this man. The doors closed before she realized her dangerous situation. The man approached her and began to touch her inappropriately. When the door opened she jumped out and ran for her room. Her youth leader met her in the hall and joined her searching for hotel security guards. In the process they spotted the offender, who responded by heading for the main door of the hotel. They followed in hot pursuit, finally finding a security guard as they reached the door. The offender was disappearing into the parking lot. Security guards searched the parking areas and issued a warning and a description to all the hotel personnel.

In both instances the parents of the girls were called immediately and informed of the situation. They were given full information and consulted for what they wanted to be done. Counseling and special staff escort was given to the girls until they felt more relaxed and secure.

Other intruders are less hostile, but still dangerous. The young men of the towns we visit always seem to find our group and our girls. Some of it is innocent—a casual conversation on the beach or in a store brings them to visit our girls in the evening. Usually they arrive with a couple male buddies to check us out. We are very up-front with our visitors. They are welcomed into the meeting or activities. We have staff eyes on them throughout their visit. We tell them the ground rules the girls are required to follow including the rule that no one from the group is allowed to leave the property with them.

Our girls get similar straightforward reminders from staff about leaving the

PARLEZ-VOUS FRANÇAIS?

Our holiday conference in downtown Montreal had given the students the option of snow sledding at Mount Royal Park. One of the students came rushing back to the hotel to tell me her friend Liz had crashed into a group of guys at the bottom of the hill. Her nose had met someone's knee. An ambulance came and took her to the hospital. The medical team spoke French. He had no idea what they said.

It had taken the student an hour to find me at the hotel. My hospital calls had taken an additional hour. We finally found Liz in the sixth hospital. I took the directions and caught a cab (we had come on coach buses) to the hospital. She had been sitting there for almost three hours untreated. When I arrived with the permission slip, we called her parents. Later that night I put her on a plane home.

Our safety and supervision plan was weak at best. There were staff at Mount Royal, but no one had a list of all the students or permission slips for them. Liz sat alone in the hospital in pain, untreated for three hours because I had not planned ahead for her safety.

grounds, keeping the rules, and continuing to be involved in the required activities. We try to keep our conversations with visitors upbeat and positive. This is a great opportunity for staff to talk about the purpose of the group and our faith in Jesus Christ. Sometimes it generates genuine interest. Others are driven away by it. Apparently sharing your faith in Jesus can also be effective as a security technique.

At no time should any student ever get into a vehicle with someone he or she just met. Anything their new "friend" offers to get for the young person can be provided by a staff member. The risk of an attack on our young people by a stranger should never be underestimated.

Staffing and Supervision at Hotels and Resorts

Smaller Ratio Needed. It is worth the extra cost to provide one staff leader for every three or four students at a hotel/resort setting. You can negotiate with the hotel to put one staff in every room with four students by using a roll-a-way bed or putting a sleeping bag on the floor. With some students it is smart to lock the windows and put the staff on the floor in front of the door at night. The ratio could be one-to-seven if the hotel provides adjoining rooms (and the door is left open) or if trusted student leaders are assigned to the room. When two or more junior high students are assigned to a room an adult should always be rooming with them.

Staff-Student Assignments. Assign staff to supervise their sleep groups throughout the trip. At every meeting and meal the staff person checks the attendance of his or her students. If they are not present the staff takes action to find them and get them there. The same procedure works for activities and curfew. The staff are to spend their time mixing normally and naturally with their students (not the other adults) throughout the conference/retreat and share activities with them. This not only provides relational evangelism and discipleship, but also puts staff in numerous situations where safety can be enforced quietly and effectively.

Security. Staff need written instructions about who to call (with phone numbers) in case of emergency situations. Every room should be checked by a staff supervisor shortly after curfew to verify that all students are in their assigned rooms. If anyone is missing, the supervising staff should follow a preplanned course of action. During the day students should be accounted for and under someone's supervision. On our week-long trips to Florida, some students have asked to stay at the hotel during the day rather than go to the beach. We assigned staff to stay with the students, and we gave them a written list with the names of the students and their room numbers. They kept contact with them during the day and watched for any violation of our rules.

Staff Team Spirit. Although everyone is assigned to certain groups of students, all the staff must be willing to approach any student who needs some supervision. When a student is standing on a balcony ledge or throwing ice in the hall, the staff leader present should step in even if he or she doesn't know that particular young man or woman. Any correction should be done respectfully and privately. No yelling or sarcasm is necessary. Young people will respect any adult who approaches them personally (my name is . . . what's yours?) and rationally (here's why we don't want you doing that . . .).

Staying In Touch. If your group is at a large conference at which students have many options for eating out and entertainment, it is wise to set up a group check-in time once or twice a day during which every student and staff member reports to a leader individually or as a group. You don't want to go through the whole day not seeing students or knowing where they are going. More contact usually means fewer surprises and problems.

Work Camps

Most of our young people raised in church families don't need more information; they need application. The work camp has become a popular site for bringing a youth group alive in their faith. But taking young people to work in national and international settings generates special safety issues.

Preparation. These trips should not be led by amateur leaders. Find a reputable organization with a track record for successful work camp projects and link your efforts to their leadership. Let the experienced professionals do the setup work. Any local or special project that you want to undertake requires a pre-trip inspection to determine what is needed. If your group is going to a non–English speaking location, you must find reliable translators to travel with you.

Student preparation requirements include applications, release, and health forms signed and notarized by parents. If the project is outside the United States or Canada, requirements will include health exams, shots, and signed consent forms for international travel. If students are going to do carpentry work or painting it would help for them to be trained in those skills prior to the trip. Training should be mandatory for using any machines or power tools.

Parents need clear and specific information about the type of work their young people are going to do on the project. This information should be written on the consent form they sign. Parents don't like to be surprised. One church group found the young people bragging and the parents cringing at the description of the group repairing the roofs of houses in a poor neighborhood. Parents complained that their young people had no experience doing that kind of work and should not have been on the roofs without safety training. The kids had a great time, but the parents were probably right.

Staying Healthy. Work teams must take special precautions to stay healthy at work sites nationally and internationally. Here are some tips groups have learned during their travels.

1. Bring plenty of sunscreen and a hat. Sunburn can incapacitate you for several days. Take caution. The purpose of the trip is to help others, not sunbathe. Do not work without a shirt or in a skimpy top. Any trip that takes you farther south than where you live puts you in hotter sun than you are used to

feeling. Drink plenty of fluids, especially when working in hot, sunny weather (see #5).

2. In foreign countries, do not go swimming in fresh water without first asking your missionary host. Some Third World countries have parasites that enter your body through your skin.

3. Do not walk around in bare feet at any time. Boots should be worn at all times. Give special attention to lacing and tying your boots. If you are asked to dig in the dirt with your hands, wear gloves. Hookworm (a type of parasite) enters the body through the skin. Dirt under your fingernails can get into your mouth and enter your system. Dress like workers, not like tourists or sunbathers. Be sensitive to the customs and dress standards of the country where you work.

4. In foreign countries, do not eat any fruits or vegetables which you cannot boil or peel (such as bananas and oranges). Do not eat anything without washing it and peeling it.

5. Always ask your host about the source and condition of the water. If the water is bad, you cannot use it even to brush your teeth or have it as ice in your drinks.

6. Expect to get diarrhea. Even the slight changes in traveling to other parts of the United States or Canada can cause intestinal disturbances. Control diarrhea with Kaopectate, Parapectolin (prescription needed), and Lomotil (prescription needed).

7. Every team member must have an updated tetanus shot. Other shots which may be required for entrance to foreign countries are typhoid, typhus, cholera, yellow fever, and gamma globulin (to prevent hepatitis). Antimalarial pills may also be required.

8. If you have allergies or any medical condition, bring the medication you will need.

9. Be careful in tropical environments. Never antagonize animals or insects that could harm you. Tarantulas and scorpions are not usually deadly, but they can seriously hurt a person. Black widow spiders, fire ants, and killer bees are very danger-

ous. Treat them with respect.

10. Immediately treat any broken skin or laceration. Infection spreads much more quickly in tropical environments.

11. Eat light to moderate amounts when eating a native meal in another country. Don't eat new types of food excessively.

12. Many travelers eat yogurt with an active culture every day for two weeks prior to an overseas trip. It may help prepare your digestive track for the different foods you will eat during the trip.

13. If anyone becomes sick, separate them from the group for at least 24 hours. Place them in a special "sick" room. Only the staff leader should be allowed to visit them and bring food, medicine, and other supplies. If the person is truly sick, the isolation will protect the team and provide the individual with privacy and quiet for sleep. If the person is just complaining to get out of work, 24 hours in isolation will change his or her mind and will discourage whining and complaining.

Equipment and Training. Many groups require power tools to be used by only adults. No student should use power tools without proper training in safety. They must show knowledge of safety and demonstrate good safety practices. The use of power tools should always require eye protection and the watchful eye of a trained adult leader. Remember parents need prior knowledge of these activities.

Cultural Awareness. Two girls on a recent work trip to Jamaica ignored the warning of their leader and broke the no smoking rule. When they disappeared from the group to light up a cigarette they stumbled into a police drug trap. They had picked up a pack of cigarettes off the ground which contained marijuana joints. They were immediately apprehended by the local police. It took hours for the trip leaders to get the girls released. When in a foreign country, stay with a national guide and leader who knows the language and the customs. Listen and learn.

Dealing with Accidents. Anticipate accidents and prevent

them before they happen. Young people will take chances. It is their nature. They often will not think ahead and look for danger. Lacking experience, they put themselves in dangerous positions. The leader must be there to correct and protect these eager young people.

When a young person is injured or becomes ill, the leader is wise to go to the maximum effort seeking treatment. On a trip to the Caribbean a young lady complained of stomach pains. A trip to the hospital brought the diagnosis of appendicitis. The leader spent much time on the phone with the parents back home, sharing all information so they could make the decision. The group had a nurse with them for the trip (always a smart idea) who helped interpret what the doctors were recommending. The young girl was flown back to the United States for additional examination before proceeding with the operation. That was what the parents wanted. The crisis was handled intelligently and carefully.

A young man was struck in the eye with a piece of sheet metal during a Hurricane Andrew cleanup trip to south Florida. The staff took him to the hospital for immediate help and continued to check on him every couple hours when they arrived back at the camp. The student told the staff everything was fine. At the same time he was telling his mother a different story about the condition of the eye. When the alarmed mother contacted the staff and demanded action, the staff leaders did not respond defensively or in anger. They did what the mother 600 miles away wanted done. Smart move.

What overnight trips are you planning for your youth group this year? Regardless of your destination or the amount of comfort your accommodations will provide, the key to a safe trip is advance planning, effective training of staff, and immediate response to problems by the youth leader. Be diligent and give significant time to discussing and preparing for safety concerns. The motto of experienced camp leaders stresses a commitment to thorough preparation: "You get what you inspect, not what you expect."

WHERE ARE THE LEADERS?

Ninety-two teenagers and 26 staff poured out of the buses and headed for the entrance gates to Disney World. Everyone knew they were to be back at the parking lot by 10 P.M. But where would they be all day?

At 11 A.M., Charlene, a volunteer leader, heard an announcement on the loudspeaker asking for a leader from their group to report to the health center. Always wanting to be helpful, she responded to the call, expecting to see other leaders there ahead of her. Instead she was the only one to respond. Heather, a teen from their group, had a high fever and felt quite sick. Charlene was glad to stay with Heather for a while until a professional leader arrived. Charlene and Heather spent the entire day in the Disney Health Center waiting for a staff leader to respond to the announcement.

It didn't have to be that way. The other leaders swore they never heard the announcement. That's probably true. Charlene made the right move staying with Heather, but it sure killed her day at Disney World.

On the next visit the staff rented three or four beepers and gave the contact number (on paper) to all the students. Now if there is any problem, the staff get beeped. They work out a team solution that meets the needs of the young person without all the burden being on one leader. In a serious emergency the head of the staff team will be just a beep away. Thanks, Charlene! We hope it won't happen again!

CHAPTER SEVEN
Summer and Winter Water Sports

All week we had played that Beach Boy music real loud at the meetings of our winter camp on the east coast of Florida. Unfortunately for three days the water had been absolutely flat. The surf boards and boogie boards we brought from New York had not ridden a single wave.

The last beach day of our trip the wind shifted around to the east and blew in a storm off the ocean. While most of our students scattered for shelter from the rain and wind, our surfer wannabes ran right past the life guard and straight into the ocean now churning with 8- to 10-foot waves.

Within minutes our guys (and gals) were getting tossed in every direction by the waves. They ignored the lifeguard's whistle signaling them to get out of the water. Our staff had a strange mixture of reactions. Yes, it was dangerous, but this *was* their last day to have the kind of ocean fun we had promised them. If they were crazy enough to be in the water in the middle of this storm, how could we stop them?

When the storm subsided we had not lost anyone. Several guys had "raspberry scrapes" on their backs and shoulders from being slammed into the sand by powerful waves. Others told about how scared they had been when the waves were turning them like a dryer in a laundromat. As we stood silently and watched our students surf through the storm, we wondered if we should have stepped in and ordered them out of the water.

Water Safety

Is water recreation a real danger or just a perceived risk? According to the National Safety Council, about 6,000 Americans drown every year. Only motor vehicle accidents and falls cause more accidental deaths. Drownings are the result of boating accidents, swimming activities, and accidental falls into water. In wilderness settings 85 percent of fatal accidents involve water.

Some of us relax around water and feel comfortable utilizing various types of water recreation activities in our youth ministry. Others see water as a dangerous element of God's creation and give it the utmost respect. This chapter surveys several popular water recreation activities and raises safety concerns related to youth ministry.

Water Safety Standards

The American Camping Association (ACA) requires camps offering aquatic programs to meet strict standards of certification for their water safety staff. How does your youth ministry measure up to these standards when you conduct a water recreation event?

Who Is the Lifeguard? Are you protected by a lifeguard who is certified through American Red Cross Lifeguard training or YMCA Lifeguard or Lifeguard BSA or Royal Lifesaving Bronze Medallion? Have the lifeguards demonstrated skill in rescue and emergency procedures specific to their situations? Are they trained and supervised to enforce established safety regulations, provide necessary instruction, identify and manage environmental and other hazards related to the activity?

Who Has Emergency Response Skills? Is there a staff person present and accessible who holds the following certifications: American Red Cross Standard First Aid or its equivalent, and cardiopulmonary resuscitation (CPR) for the age level certified by the American Red Cross, The American Heart Association, or the equivalent?

What Preparations Have You Made?

● Have you listed specific safety rules for the water-related activity? Do you orient all the students to the safety rules and procedures prior to the activity?

● Do you have written procedures for emergency and accident responses? Are these procedures rehearsed periodically?

● Are students tested for swimming ability before they are allowed to participate in aquatic activities?

● Do the lifeguards and lookouts have a system that enables them to quickly account for all participants?

● Is rescue equipment readily available and in good condition?

The best water safety preparation we can make in youth ministry is to have our youth swim under the supervision of a certified lifeguard. As an adult leader we must defer to the judgment and leadership of the lifeguard in matters of water safety and support him or her before our students. When we operate without a certified lifeguard, we take the heavy responsibility of safety upon ourselves. In either situation, the general rules of swimming safety apply.

Safety Tips for Swimming

● Know your swimming abilities. Don't test yourself or others in situations beyond your skills.

● Never swim alone. Use a buddy system.

● Never swim close to any areas designated for sail or motor boats.

● Never dive until you are sure the water is sufficiently deep and the bottom is free of hazardous objects.

● Don't use flotation devices or water toys which might allow you to be carried far out into deep water.

● Never try to swim against a strong current. Drift with it and swim diagonally across it.

● When caught in an undertow (shorter and deeper than a

current) turn and go with it swimming a diagonal course to the surface.

- After sunset, swim only in well-lighted areas.
- At the first flash of lightning, exit the water immediately.
- Follow instructions from lifeguards. Respect their decisions. Never fake an emergency.

If there are students in your youth ministry who cannot swim, a lasting gift to them for life would be to teach them. Make a goal to have every student in your group become a competent swimmer. In addition, encourage some of your student leaders to take the lifeguard training offered by the Red Cross or YMCA. These organizations could provide your group top quality safety coverage while developing their life skills.

Using Private and Public Pools
Public pools with certified lifeguards on duty make your safety job easy. Private pools in the homes of your friends or youth group members put the safety responsibility back into your hands.

- Never allow swimming unattended by a trained adult.
- Forbid running, pushing, and fighting around the pool.
- Beware of the diving board. Use it cautiously.
- Don't overload the pool.
- Don't allow students to jump on top of others.
- Forbid chicken fighting (riding on a person's shoulders).
- Don't allow anyone to be held under water.
- Keep electrical devices away from the pool. Make sure electrical outlets are equipped with ground-fault switches.
- Keep emergency response equipment and phone numbers accessible.

Using Lakes and Ponds
- Never allow swimming unattended by a trained adult.
- Check the bottom for hazardous debris.
- Have a designated swimming area.
- Don't allow diving without first checking the depth of the water.

- Beware of pushing or fighting on the rafts.
- Know where to get emergency assistance.

Swimming in the Ocean

- Swim only under the supervision of a lifeguard. Swim near the lifeguard stand.
- Stay away from piers and pilings.
- Look out for dangerous aquatic life (jellyfish, stinging coral, etc.).
- Don't try to swim against strong currents. To make it back to shore, swim gradually away from the current.
- Follow the instructions of the lifeguards regarding surf conditions.

Canoeing/Rafting/Tubing

For the best results and the safest conditions in these activities, find a reputable outfitter and arrange for the equipment, training, and supervision you need. The conditions can vary widely from flat, slow moving water to a fast, rapid-filled river. Obviously, the deeper and faster the water the greater the risk.

Canoeing Safety Checklist

- Wear personal flotation devices (life jackets) at all times. Cushions are not reliable. Personal flotation devices safe for use must be U.S. Coast Guard-approved and of the proper type, size, and fit for each user.
- The flotation devices must be worn snug and tight. Loose flotation devices are dangerous because they can hold a person underwater.
- Be sure everyone in the canoes can swim.
- Notify several people or officials about your trip route and estimated return.
- Stick to the route you planned. If you were to have an accident or trouble, rescuers or other people would have difficulty finding you if you changed your plans.
- In wilderness country, don't be caught without a map or magnetic compass. Islands and lakes look alike. Portage trails

seem to disappear if you don't watch the signs carefully.

● Never run a stretch of rapids or white water without knowing exactly what lies ahead. Walk along the fast stretch to check the conditions before you attempt to run the river. If you have the least doubt you can't make it safely, portage the canoes.

● Never stand up in a canoe. It is safer to change places by going ashore to do so.

● Carry a properly stocked first-aid kit. Know how to use it.

● Be sure your canoe is in proper balance. Don't overload it. The middle section of the canoe should be at least six inches above the water line.

● Always keep a bailing can aboard and a large size sponge to remove the excess water on the bottom of the canoe.

● If you are caught in a squall, sit in the bottom of the canoe; if conditions warrant it, lie flat on the bottom in such a position that you can bail.

● If the canoe capsizes, hold on to the canoe and kick-swim it to shore. Canoes are buoyant and will float. It is safer to stay with the craft than to attempt to swim ashore.

● Learn how to right an upset canoe in the water. Learn how to reenter a swamped canoe.

● At the first sign of lightning get out of the water and away from your metal canoe. Wait out the storm in a nearby shelter or under small trees.

● Avoid swinging the canoe paddles to splash another canoe.

● Avoid paddling across a long straight course across a lake because storms can blow up quickly. Stay close to shore.

● Have a staff member present who holds the following certifications: American Red Cross Standard First Aid or the equivalent and cardiopulmonary resuscitation for the age level served from the American Red Cross, The American Heart Association, or the equivalent.

In a Deep, Fast River
In white water, all canoeists should wear helmets to protect their heads from rocks and debris if their craft should capsize. They

should not be in the water downstream from their canoe. The water will push the canoe toward them with tremendous force. If they become pinned against something in the river, the canoe could do great injury to them. Take great caution when trees and branches are down in the river. Canoeists in and out of their canoes can be pushed into these obstructions by the force of the river and held there, causing hypothermia or drowning.

Staff Supervision of a Canoe Trip

The maximum size for a controlled canoe trip is 8 to 12 canoes (with two people in each canoe). Three or four leaders or guides should be assigned to specific positions throughout the canoes. One leader should be at the front. No canoe should be allowed to pass the leader's canoe. In the middle of the group should be two experienced leaders in canoes supervising and monitoring the students in the canoes. The fourth leader should stay in the rear of the group to act as a sweeper and to insure everyone's safe passage.

The leaders should be selected on the basis of their canoeing experience, their knowledge of the river, and their demonstrated ability to control a group of four canoes (eight young people). In each leader's canoe should be a first aid kit and a set of ropes with ring buoys which can be thrown to people as lifelines. It is best to take the leaders on a pre-trip run down the river to build their knowledge of the river and give them experience communicating with each other while they are actually canoeing.

Pre-Trip Training

A pre-trip training in an indoor facility is highly recommended for students as well as staff. Make the pool training part of the whole trip package. Lay out the rules of the trip. Use the life jackets and the paddles. Give basic instruction in all aspects of canoeing including stroking and righting a capsized canoe. The pool setting provides opportunity to test swimming skills and teach safety techniques in a controlled setting. The training process gives insight into the teachable attitude of each student.

The pool training may eliminate some students from the trip. If they cannot take instruction in the pool, don't expect them to cooperate when everyone is moving down a river.

Water Sports Warning

Youth leaders should not sign a group waiver form and take responsibility for all the students. When the river company or outfitter requires waiver's releasing them from responsibility, get the forms prior to the trip. Give the forms to the students to be signed and notarized by the parents.

In a lawsuit that is still pending, a youth leader and the ministry he is employed by is being sued by the family of a young person who was killed during a rafting trip. The leader signed the waiver form for the river company at the site just before they left on the trip. His signature said he and his ministry organization would take responsibility for the students. Lack of planning and a spur-of-the-moment decision caused the youth leader to take the responsibility that belonged only to the parents. He and his ministry are awaiting the judgment of the courts.

Rafting and Tubing

Whitewater rafting has gotten a great deal of scrutiny from the insurance industry because of several fatal tragedies. Although these accidents were on dangerous Class V rivers, every rafting outfitter has been placed under the same scrutiny. The job of the youth leader is to find a top notch outfitter with good equipment to guide the youth group.

Many of the safety guidelines listed above for canoeing apply to rafting. Listen to the instructions of your outfitter. Let the company do the work and provide the safety precautions for which you are paying.

Be sure to check the liability insurance policy of your church or youth ministry to see if it excludes whitewater rafting. Work with the outfitter to make sure each participant is adequately covered with insurance.

Tubing should be confined to slow, lazy rivers on hot summer days. It is impossible to control a tube or protect arms and legs (and butt) in a fast river with rocks. Even with a helmet, the risk of injury is beyond what is acceptable for a youth ministry. Even in the slow river everyone must be a strong swimmer. The staff must know the river (is there a waterfall ahead?) and be strategically placed throughout the group as specified in the canoeing instructions.

Water Skiing/Boating

Late in the afternoon at a Christian camp a full-time, experienced water safety staff member broke his own rules of safety. He had been driving the water ski boat for over four hours (rule #1) and was feeling the fatigue. This last ride was a good friend who was asking for more and more challenges. He accommodated the requests of his friend (rule #2) and took him off the normal ski course. He drove the boat into an area of the lake restricted to sail boats (rule #3) and crashed the water ski boat directly into a sail boat.

WHAT CAUSES WATER ACCIDENTS

- Alcohol and drug use while participating in water recreation
- Diving into unknown waters or water that is too shallow
- Overestimating ability and stamina
- Sudden immersion (falls into water)
- Accidents involving small boats
- Medical emergencies, such as heart attacks and seizures

American Red Cross

The occupants of the sail boat had seen him coming and had dived off the boat into the water. A young woman from the sail boat was just ascending to the surface when the propeller of the motor boat passed her. The young woman sustained deep lacerations to her back. The water safety staff member immediately stopped the boat and switched into the emergency response mode in which he had been so thoroughly trained. Miraculously the young woman lived and recovered.

Following the accident the camp staff review determined that the highly trained, mature leader driving the boat had been the victim of fatigue. He was so familiar with the water front situation that he overlooked the risks of skiing outside the designated areas. Familiarity had bred contempt for the risk. He got caught up in the moment of a relationship with a friend who wanted to push the limits of his skiing ability. It was a lapse of maturity on the leader's part to accommodate his friend.

The staff leader bears a resemblance to many youth ministry people. He was diligent and hard working. He had been in the driver's seat four hours without relief. He was like most youth ministers—highly motivated and not able to know when to quit.

He was also highly relational, eager to meet any request of a friend. All together in this situation his strengths became his weakness. Fortunately for him the young woman's remarkable recovery freed him from carrying an enormous weight of guilt the rest of his life.

Boating Safety

If a mature professional can experience a safety lapse, it serves as a warning to the rest of us who use boats only occasionally throughout the year. If your youth ministry is going to use a boat for some activities, you are responsible to make sure it meets basic safety requirements.

You may be looking at a boat owned by a camp you are using or a borrowed boat loaned to you for youth ministry use. Check the boat and the driver before you trust your students to step on board.

Boating Safety Checklist

- Know the capabilities of your boat and motor.
- Know your fuel tank capacity. Monitor frequently so not to be stranded.
- Don't overload your boat. Balance your load.
- Have firefighting and lifesaving equipment always ready for use.
- Obey all boating laws and regulations.
- Have personal flotation devices for every person in the boat. This is the law.
- All children must wear life preservers. Everyone must wear them in rough weather.
- Prepare for emergency routines—fire, man overboard, bad leaks, motor breakdown, storm, etc.

- Learn distress and other marine signals
- Carry proper charts and a magnetic compass.
- Have at least one person on board prepared to serve as emergency co-pilot.
- Follow manufacturer's specifications for the number of passengers to carry safely.
- Make sure that everyone in the boat is seated before the motor is started.
- Drive at less-than-average speeds in unfamiliar waters to reduce the possibility of striking an unexpected obstacle.
- Watch for swimmers.
- Know the official storm signals. Boat accordingly.
- When it appears that a storm is possible, head for home without delay.
- Angle your boat toward high waves and reduce speed.
- Avoid unnecessarily fast, sharp turns. Don't take the risk of being swamped or capsized by high waves.
- If the boat capsizes, passengers should try to stay with it. The overturned boat can support quite a few people even if it is nearly underwater.
- In an emergency situation guard against panic. Calmness, cooperation, and resourcefulness are required for survival.

Water Skiing Safety Considerations

Waterskiing is a popular special activity in many youth ministries. It gives opportunity to build relationships while sharing an exhilarating sports experience. It is most safely operated in the context of an accredited camp. Other youth ministries use boats periodically in local settings. In a variation to involve more kids, the boats also pull young people on knee boards and inflated inner tubes. The following safety considerations apply to all these variations.

- Know and follow the state laws governing boating and skiing.
- Ski in safe areas, free from shallow rocks and undesirable obstructions.
- Load the ski boat with enough forward ballast to hold

down the bow and guarantee forward vision. The safety of the skier depends entirely upon where the boat takes him or her.

• Always have a trained adult spotter in the boat to watch the skier and communicate with the driver. Many states now also require the boat to have a rear view mirror in addition to a spotter. Check your state's requirements.

• Insist that all skiers wear legal life jackets. Know what the law requires.

• Review and use a standard set of signals for communications between boat and skier.

• Remember that the boat can slow down faster than the skier can.

• When terminating a run, slow down gradually before cutting the engine to protect the skier from being driven into the boat by his or her momentum.

• Watch for swimmers and other hazards when skiing near a beach. Stay away from congested shore areas.

• Avoid towing skiers through heavily traveled or congested areas.

• Teach skiers to grab one ski and hold it vertically out of the water when they fall so that other boats can see them in the water. Do the same with a knee board.

• Stop the boat motor (don't just switch to neutral) when taking a skier aboard.

• Never tow your skier through shallow waters at high speeds. A tumble could be hazardous.

• Never tow two or more tubes or kneeboards with students of significantly different weights or with different lengths of rope. The longer rope can decapitate the person holding on to the shorter rope.

• Terminate water skiing well before twilight when visibility decreases.

• Inspect tow lines and fastenings regularly for worn or damaged equipment.

Water Safety Training
The American Red Cross, YMCA, YWCA, and other organizations offer water safety courses and comprehensive training for

SummerandWinterWaterSports117

leaders and individuals. Textbooks and practical instruction will give leaders confidence in handling safety procedures and emergency responses around water activities.

You can contact the local office of these organizations in your community or the national headquarters listed in the appendix of this book.

Winter Water Sports (Skating, Sledding, and Skiing)

"Wake up, Jack! Steven is hurt. He ran into the tree and he can't move." I couldn't decide if the voice was coming from my dreams or from reality. I opened my eyes to see ski jackets and mittens hovering over me begging me to get up and come with them. I asked Steven's location. I sent one young man to wake another counselor from the group (I was just a weekend visitor). I gave the students a blanket to wrap around Steven. I cautioned them not to move him but to tell him I would be there as soon as I got dressed.

What time was it? I squinted through my sleepy eyes to see 3:00 A.M. glaring back at me. I knew I had to dress for cold weather. The temperature had been barely above zero degrees Fahrenheit all weekend. It had to be at least 15 degrees below zero now. I prayed for Steven as I dressed and asked God to show me what I needed to do when I arrived at the scene of the accident.

When I walked out of the camp dormitory to the sledding hill, I was surprised to find no one at the hill or near the tree where they told me Steven was lying. After searching the area, I returned to the building to find Steven in his bed, surrounded by a roomful of kids. He had been sledding with all of them 3 A.M. while the counselors were sound asleep. He had hit the tree head first. The impact caused a temporary paralysis which made it impossible for him to move for a few minutes. When the feeling returned he had gotten up off the ground and walked to his room.

As Steven lay in his bunk, he was sore, scared, and thankful the paralysis wasn't permanent. I was quite aggravated about the 3 A.M. sledding, but I was glad he wasn't still lying on the ground next to that tree. The discussion turned to Steven's need to visit the hospital emergency room for a checkup. He said he was fine. That was teen speak for "I don't want to explain to my parents why I was sledding at 3 A.M." He almost had a couple of the counselors convinced until I stepped in and demanded he be taken to the hospital. To my amazement, Steven suffered no serious damage or any side effects.

When the temperature drops and the water turns to snow and ice, youth ministry activities become even more exciting. Snow camps, winter retreats, ski trips, and ice-skating parties help youth groups enjoy the cold weather. The safety factors for winter activities become intense because the winter weather creates an environment filled with fast and slippery hard surfaces surrounded by cold temperatures.

Ice

Ice skating is popular with youth groups year round, for many can go to indoor arenas. In most situations the level of safety is acceptable because of the regulations and supervision provided by the operators of the rink. When the youth ministry moves away from the rink and on to the pond or lake, keeping kids safe becomes more challenging.

● Check the thickness of the ice. The Red Cross suggests that for maximum safety, the ice should be at least four inches thick. Check the entire area you intend to use for sufficient thickness. The more people you put on the ice the thicker it needs to be. Mark off as restricted areas any sections where the ice is not sufficiently thick.

● Look for objects or other hazards that stick out above the ice. Mark them so they can be avoided.

● Always have something you can use to throw or extend to a person who has fallen though the ice. It could be a long pole or a lifeline with a buoy. Prepare for the worst and hope you never have to use such devices.

● If the ice starts to crack, lie down flat on the ice, spreading your hands and legs far apart to distribute your weight across a wide area. Crawl toward the safer, thicker ice maintaining your prone, spread position. Do not stand up until you are safely on solid ground.

How to Help Someone Who Has Fallen through the Ice

● Don't go out onto the ice to help. You may join the person in the cold water if you do. Extend an emergency device which the victim can grasp and hold onto. Use a long pole, a tree branch, a buoy on a life line, or an inner tube attached to a rope.

● Get something to the person to grasp quickly. The longer the victim is in the cold water, the less he or she will be able to function. Pull the victim to shore or get the victim attached to the rescue device and go for help.

● Coach the victim to remain calm and to reach forward onto the ice, using a swimming type kick to push himself up on the ice. He should stay prone on the ice, distributing his weight, then crawl or roll away from the hole in the ice.

● Get the victim into dry clothes and warm shelter as quickly as possible. Warm the person with a warm (not hot) shower or bath, or near a fire. Give the person warm liquids, but avoid alcohol or caffeine. Wrap them in dry clothes, a blanket, or sleeping bag. Get medical assistance if possible.

More Ice Problems

Many youth ministers believe that games on ice are even more fun than on solid ground. It is not unusual to see broom hockey, ice hockey, football, soccer, and all types of relay races on ice. The problem is the surface of ice—it is just like concrete. When young people fall, the damage will likely be great. If the professional hockey leagues require helmets for safety of the players, should less-coordinated students participate in contact sports on ice without head protection? Even with helmets, the students face a greater risk of broken bones playing on ice.

Fun in the Snow

We were promoting our winter snow camp with a film piece that showed more than 20 people sliding down a snow covered trail in the woods on 10 to 12 inner tubes that had been lashed together. It was like a raft trip through the woods over the snow. It looked like so much fun.

When we arrived at our camp, we were excited to duplicate what we had seen on the film. The camp had the snow, the inner tubes, and the long, downhill runs. The camp director assigned one of his professional staff to our tube run to supervise our activities. His rules were much different than what we expected or wanted. He allowed only one person on the tube at a time and only one tube on the course at a time. He placed some spotters on the course and at the bottom to help the rider exit the course and return up the hill. It seemed as if he was spoiling all the fun. In fact, when he would be called away for some task around the camp, we would defy the younger camp counselors and hook three or four tubes together, pile as many people on them as possible and take a merry ride down the hill. It seemed like a lot more fun.

Since that weekend we have used many camps where there has been no professional supervision. We have had total freedom to do whatever we wanted with tubes, sled, and toboggans. Left to our own rules, we have discovered our camp director friend was pretty smart.

Most accidents on tubes, sleds, and toboggans happen when people hit other people—a body crashing into other bodies. You pile two people on top of a tube for a run down the hill. It is great fun until a bump sends one person's head into the teeth of his fellow passenger or the bulk of one rider lands full force on an arm or a skinny leg of the other rider. We loved to play chicken with the people standing in the runway of the track. We hated to wait for people to clear the track.

Most of our accidents and hospital runs, however, were caused by people hitting others either deliberately or because they were out of control. We loved to spin people on the tubes and send them down backwards, but we have seen people hit trees and other people because they had no idea of where they were headed and had no ability to change direction.

You have to ask yourself if it is worth the risk of injury to continue a no-restraints approach to tubes, toboggans, and sleds. It is impossible to safety-proof tobogganing, sledding, and tubing in the snow. Although most of us have done these activities since we were kids, a safety check points out that accidents happen because of the speed, the lack of control, and the exposure of arms, legs, and heads to collisions. For the best possible safety follow these guidelines:

• Have a straight, wide course free of hazards and obstructions (including people).

• Avoid using sleds and toboggans with metal runners or metal facing which could cut someone's skin.

• Allow just one rider on each tube and sled. Don't overload large toboggans. Have all riders head down the hill feet first.

• Place staff leaders at the top and bottom of the hill to spot for the students and to enforce the rules.

• Discourage the building of jumps on the run. Being lifted in the air is fun, but landing on the ground is dangerous.

Snowmobiles

Snowmobiles are excluded from many insurance policies because of the loose restrictions concerning their operation and the numerous accidents involving them. Many camps still run snowmobiles under their own insurance policies, allowing only qualified camp staff to operate the powerful vehicles. Helmets should always be worn. Safety precautions should be taken by both the driver and the rider.

In an attempt to be creative, some camps pull campers on inner tubes water ski style. The terrain, though, is less predictable than a water surface. During the research for this book, several youth leaders reported that young people from their group had hit trees when they were on tubes pulled by snowmobiles. One student suffered brain damage. Check your insurance policy before using snowmobiles. If you have coverage, use only qualified drivers, wear helmets, and obey safety regulations.

Downhill Skiing

A youth organization recently had an embarrassing day in the legal system. They were being sued by the family of a young man who had sustained a serious back injury while downhill skiing with their group. What was unique about this legal proceeding was that the episode in question was recorded on video tape shot by one of the youth group leaders.

The video clearly showed the young man was a novice skier trying to ski down a slope that was beyond his capabilities. He was skiing out of control and fell, injuring his back. The students and staff skiing with him could be heard encouraging him to ski down this slope and laughing when he fell. As he lay on the snow they quipped and joked with him about getting up to continue skiing. In the context of the accident, the comments took on a different tone than was perhaps intended. The leaders sounded insensitive and unconcerned for his safety. The judgment of the suit went against the youth organization.

A responsible skiing trip starts with staff preparations. The leader needs release forms and medical information for all the participants. It is smart to have at least one alternate driver riding with you in case one of the drivers suffers an injury during the day. If you are skiing several hours from home, trying to find another capable driver could be costly in dollars and time. Each person in your group should be given a slip of paper with your name and the name of your group which can be used by emergency personnel if they call for leaders over a public address system. Ski trips often attract many students who don't know the group or the leaders very well. They might not be able to identify who is responsible for them when they are asked by medical personnel.

Set a meeting time during the day (a 60-minute period) when everyone should report to a staff person at a designated location. Set a quitting time and a meeting spot for departure. If possible, have an adult at a designated location throughout the day. Show students the location and tell them to come to this person if they need any help during the day. That adult should also know how to contact the leader during the day if necessary.

If you travel by bus, have alternate transportation available if it is necessary to take a student to an emergency room.

Instruct your students not to ski alone. Try to establish small groups of skiers to stay with each other and look out for each other. Try to get adult leaders spread out into all the various groups of skiers. Be sure that capable adult leaders are supervising the beginning skiers.

In extremely cold weather, instruct your students to return to the lodge to warm up after a certain period of time or number of runs. Alert students to the signs of frostbite and warn them to get help from you or the infirmary before they develop a severe condition.

Make sure that all skiers wear goggles to protect their eyes from snow and ice and from damage caused by the sun.

Don't let any of your experienced skiers take other students on to ski trails that are beyond their skiing skills. Review the skiing safety code. Let your experienced skiers who may find this boring do the presentation to the group.

Skier's Responsibility Code

1. Ski under control and in such a manner that you can stop or avoid other skiers or objects.

2. When skiing downhill or overtaking another skier, you must avoid the skier below you.

3. Do not stop where you obstruct a trail or are not visible from above.

4. When entering a trail or starting downhill, yield to other skiers.

5. Wear retention straps or other devices to help prevent runaway skis.

6. Keep off closed trails and posted areas and observe all posted signs.

Four Major Causes of Skiing Injuries

Instruction. The goal of skiing instruction is to teach skiers how to control where they are going, how fast they are going, and how to stop. Every beginning skier needs instruction. The responsible leader must provide that instruction either through professional lessons at the lodge's ski school or from capable volunteers in the youth group. Most of the injuries at a ski mountain happen to beginning skiers. Many of those injuries occur on ski slopes that are much more challenging than the skiers are able to handle. It is important to take the necessary time to teach young people to ski under control. They cannot be taken to the top of the mountain and turned loose to learn on their own. The throw-'em-in-the-deep-end method of teaching people to swim or ski is much too risky for a youth ministry leader.

Once I took a young man skiing who had never skied before. I was impatient and didn't want to spend all morning on the bunny slope. He was young and athletic. I was confident I could teach him on the way down the hill. Looking at the trail map, I found some green trails (easiest) on the side of the mountain. When we left the chair lift at the top of the mountain, I discovered the green trails were closed. I was angry, but I had not taken time to check the condition of the trails before I took this novice skier up on the chair lift.

Now I was at the top of the lift with a young man who never skied before. Only blue (difficult) and black (expert) trails were open. The trip down was a real disaster for him. Falling constantly took the energy and confidence out of him. After 15 minutes he hated skiing. After he took a nasty fall, I realized the danger I had put him in and flagged down a ski patrol. They called a sled to take him down to the base of the mountain and gave me a well-deserved reprimand. We spent the rest of the day on the bunny slope rebuilding his confidence and teaching him the basics.

The same pressure is applied to many young people by their friends who have more skiing experience. They don't want to spend the day on the bunny slope. They forget what it takes to learn to ski. They take their friends into danger, accidents happen, and someone gets hurt. The leader then gets to spend the rest of the day in the first aid station or at the hospital emergency room. Prevent these accidents by demanding your new skier stay on the bunny slope until he or she demonstrates an ability to ski under control.

Physical Conditioning. Learning to ski can be very hard on some young people who are not physically fit. Not everyone is ready for the rigors of skiing. Weaker people sustain more injuries. Strong leg muscles and ligaments are needed to withstand the forces of a fall. Stamina is needed to keep you from tiring quickly. Either prepare your nonathletes prior to the trip, or keep a staff leader nearby to monitor them while they ski.

Equipment. Good equipment which is properly fitted and adjusted reduces the possibilities of injury. Resist the temptation to save equipment rental money by borrowing equipment for new skiers. The fit of the boots, the length of the skis and poles, and the release setting on the bindings are crucial to safety and comfort. When young people rent equipment, remind them to be honest about two questions they will be asked—their weight and their skiing ability. Their answers will determine how tightly the bindings holding the boots to the skis will be tightened. They shouldn't be embarrassed or pressured into giving information that isn't true. A dishonest answer can result in a broken leg

BORROWED EQUIPMENT

Cliff thought borrowing skis from a neighbor was a great way to save money for the youth group ski trip. The skis had not been used for quite a few years, but they looked good to him. He felt special when he showed up at the departure point with his own pair of skis.

Fortunately Cliff had a leader who knew skiing. He praised Cliff for his effort to find some skis, but cautioned him about their safety. First they were 195mm length, taller than Cliff, who as a beginner probably needed 160mm skis. Second the bindings were set so tight that the leader could not hammer the boots off when they were set in place. Cliff would have snapped the bones in his leg during his first bad fall because the boots would have stayed attached to the skis.

If students are using borrowed ski equipment, have it checked with someone who knows ski equipment and safety prior to the trip. Don't let someone hurt himself trying to save money.

when the ski doesn't release properly from the boot when the skier falls.

Lack of Sound Judgment. Beginners have little conception of how great a hazard speed can be. They often overestimate their abilities and are deaf to instructions. The key to safety is skiing under control. Most accident victims tell the same basic story. "I just started going faster and faster. I didn't know how to stop." Or "My skis got crossed and I couldn't control where they were going."

The lack of sound judgment also causes people to ski past the point of exhaustion. The last run of the day is notorious for accidents. Skiers become fatigued and grow careless or unable to control their speed. Be careful not to verbally abuse the youth in your group when they say they are tired or want to quit for the day. Your comments may push them to ski beyond their physical limits. The leader bears some responsibility for any accidents to students not given an opportunity to rest or call it quits.

After a full day of skiing with a group of young people the trip home offers some additional safety challenges. The parking lot of the ski area can be hazardous. Tired students with aching feet don't always pay close attention to the traffic. Vehicles with snow or winter dirt on the windshield don't always have clear visibility. The light of the late afternoon is fading. People are standing by their vehicles changing clothes and loading equipment. Give special attention to your group and to others around you to avoid any parking lot mishaps. Be sure your driver for the trip home is alert and rested.

CHAPTER EIGHT
High Adventure

Lenny slammed his bicycle down on the pavement of the roadside parking lot. Walking quickly by the picnic table covered with sandwiches and drinks, he cursed everyone and everything in his path. Just two-and-a-half days into an eight-day, 400-mile bicycle trip, Lenny was coming apart. Upon reaching the side entrance of the park, he announced he was going home. . . and he started walking.

I calmly ate my lunch waiting for Lenny to return. When he was almost out of sight, I realized he was serious. My legs felt like jello, but I ran down the road in pursuit. Lenny had no idea where he was or where he was going (a perfect illustration of his life). He was like a ticking time bomb rolling down the road. Nearly a mile later I finally cornered him against a barbed wire fence and attempted to calm and defuse him.

The peace treaty we negotiated was only temporary. Every day something else related to Lenny exploded. He collapsed from heat exhaustion because he insisted on riding with his jeans and jacket on. He sabotaged his own bike. He was in a fight almost every day. One incident came immediately after another student pulled Lenny out of a river when he appeared to be drowning. During a rain storm he was riding so erratically that the staff leader separated him from the rest of the group. In anger, Lenny pulled a knife and threatened him.

Before the trip, I had thought a high-adventure trip would help Lenny turn his life around. Now I wonder how we ever survived the week. Today I realize that putting Lenny in a high-adventure situation threatened not only his safety but also the well-being of all the other students and staff.

What Is High Adventure?

High adventure is voluntarily putting ourselves into situations in the physical environment that challenge our physical and emotional toughness. High adventure is doing what is outside the boundaries of what most people would consider normal, safe activities.

High adventure includes mountaineering, ballooning, scuba diving, bicycling, motorcycling, canoeing, kayaking, hang gliding, rafting, sailing, skiing, skydiving, rock climbing, trekking, and survival camping. This chapter provides some general safety principles for use in these activities by a youth ministry. Special attention is given to bicycle touring and hiking/backpacking with a short note about rock climbing and rappelling, because they are often utilized in youth ministry. Check the chapters on water activities and winter activities for additional comments.

Before Considering High Adventure

One word of advice fits all—high adventure activities are never to be attempted by anyone who lacks training and experience. The smartest move any youth leader can make is to hire a certified trainer or guide to lead the youth group through one of these activities. If you are unwilling to spend the money to hire qualified guides, stay away from these activities. Don't rush ignorantly into any high-adventure trips with a local amateur staff. It takes time to recognize the risks and develop competence and experience in your leaders.

By definition high adventure trips are risky and dangerous. That's part of the attraction that draws many youth leaders to use them. These trips are stressful on people physically, emotionally, socially, and every other way. Even when following the strictest safety standards, accidents will happen because these activities are conducted in a dangerous environment.

Questions Worth Asking

Why do I want to involve young people in high adventure? Is high adventure really necessary to accomplish your goals? The first step in planning any activity is writing a clear purpose statement for the activity. Perhaps there is a better way to accomplish your goal. Exposing your young people to the risks of high adventure may be unnecessary.

Who is going to lead this high adventure experience? Do you have the experienced and qualified leaders to safely lead this adventure or will you hire professional guides? Quality leadership is the most important ingredient for both safety and success in high adventure.

What type of young people should participate? Was it wise to bring Lenny on the bicycle trip? Definitely not. He was not ready physically, emotionally, or socially for the stress involved in a 400-mile bicycle trip with 30 of his peers. It is important to seek vital information about the young people you intend to take on high adventure.

- What is their physical health?
- What are their physical abilities and capabilities?
- Do they have drug or alcohol problems? High adventure is not the place to go cold turkey.
- Is their behavior at home irrational or unpredictable? High adventure will magnify it.
- Are they cocky, ego-driven, reckless, afraid to fail? (if so, expect severe overreaction and poor response to leadership)
- How do they act when under stress in their normal environment and routine? (the answer is a reliable guide to how they will behave in high-adventure situations)
- How well do they take instruction?
- Are there scapegoat kids in your group—targets of peer abuse?
- Is there adequate time to screen students individually and determine how this trip might affect each person?
- What training and conditioning will you provide prior to

the trip to prepare the students?

Lenny came on the trip at the last minute because I insisted on taking him. He wasn't screened with these type of questions. We didn't know until after the trip that he had been kicked out of three schools for fighting. As much as we cared, we were not prepared to help him. The situation we thrust him into only aggravated his problems. He was a major safety risk to himself and others around him.

What is our true exposure to danger through this event? Experience is vital for risk to be fairly and accurately assessed. Most dangerous situations are repetitive and can be predicted by experienced leaders. As a youth leader you must know what risks your students will face and decide if it is worth it. Those decisions are best made prior to departing, not in the heat of the moment.

What is the quality of the equipment we will use? It pays to go with a certified trained outfitter who has quality equipment. It is seldom worth the investment for your group to buy specialty items for occasional use. High adventure requires top quality equipment. This is not the place for shortcuts or budget constraints.

How do my staff and I react when we experience a trial run? Before taking any students, take yourself and your adult leaders (with a qualified guide) on a shortened sample of the high adventure experience you are considering. Seeing, feeling, and touching it for yourself will help you decide if it is best for the students you serve. Use the time to teach your leaders needed skills in group process. Debriefing experiences are the primary teaching opportunities high adventure trips offer. With the help of your staff, students can learn valuable lessons about themselves regarding pressure, people, situations, fears, and faith.

What is our insurance coverage for this activity? Don't wait until you have an accident to ask this question. Your insurance agent doesn't want to be surprised with a claim for an event your policy excludes. If you are working with a reputable outfitter, you should be able to arrange special coverage to protect everyone involved. Be sure that you have both medical and liability coverage for the trip. Seek the approval of your board or church leaders to confirm that you have sufficient insurance coverage.

Do parents know what's going on? This is key. Parents need specifics (verbally and in writing) about what their young people will be experiencing on this trip. One of the major causes of lawsuits is surprise. Parents deserve prior knowledge. Put all the information on the permission form they will sign to give their consent for the activity.

Bicycle Trips

It was always a four-star, goose-flesh experience for parents. The long double line of bicycles, each marked with a fluorescent orange flag, coasted down the paved road into the picnic area of the state park, marking the end of a 600-mile trip. Parents and relatives would rush from the picnic tables to line the road and look for that special face of their child.

The bikers would roll through a gauntlet of flash cubes, video cameras, and spirited applause before stopping to dismount and walk back into normal life. Mothers would cry. We had arrived home safely. Fathers would beam with pride (especially for their daughters). It was a memorable moment of relief and satisfaction. For me it was mostly relief.

Biking with young people has provided some of the great joys of my life and sadly, the greatest sorrow I have ever known (see chapter 11). Genuine risk is always present. Despite the most thoughtful and strict safety standards, accidents will happen. Any leader considering biking with the youth group must count the potential cost.

I understand and respect parents who do not want their son or daughter biking on a public roadway. The setting is filled with many potentially uncontrollable elements. Our goal as youth leaders is to provide such a responsible atmosphere of safety that if parents allow their son or daughter to bike on any public road at any time, they can be confident each rider is safer with our group than riding on his or her own.

Bicycling Safety Essentials

The essentials of safety remain the same in all bicycling situations when traveling on public highways. There is no difference between a two-week tour or a one-day training ride near your home; the following requirements still apply:

Leadership. As always, good leaders are the key component of safe riding. One riding leader for every three to five student riders is the best ratio. A group of six students could be adequately supervised by one junior leader (experienced college-age or less-experienced adult) and one senior leader (experienced adult).

A good leader is defined by riding experience, physical conditioning, basic leadership skills, and commitment to the standards of safety. The absence of any of these qualifications significantly raises the risk of accidents and injuries. Being responsible for the safety of biking students is not the place for on-the-job training.

Riding Group Size. Ideal size for biking is six to eight people including leaders. More people in a group creates supervision difficulties, hinders communication, and becomes a hazard to other vehicles. Larger groups are socially more fun, but significantly raise the probability of accidents. Stay small. It's safer. The size of the entire group will be determined by the number of qualified leaders you have and the capacity of your accommodations. Trips of 30–40 people seem to work best.

Safety Equipment and Preparation. Before you hit the road with your students make sure that you have the required equipment:

1. Helmets are an absolute must. Don't let anyone ride 100 feet without wearing a quality biking helmet. The highest percentage of fatal accidents in biking are caused by severe head injuries. Accept no excuses: No helmet—no riding. Check the helmet of each rider to make sure it rests squarely on the head, protecting the front portion of their head as well as the rear. All chin straps must be fastened and drawn tight when riding. The helmet should be comfortable, but the rider should not able to move it up and down or side to side on the head. You can always expect resistance from some who don't want to wear helmets properly or wear them at all. Remind them they will probably only need that helmet once during their life, but that one moment could be the difference between a long life and a short life.

2. *Orange fluorescent flags* on six foot long fiberglass poles provide added visibility in all directions. They attach with a bracket to the rear axle of the bike or can be taped to a rear carrying rack. Flags, poles, and brackets can be obtained through bike dealers or major discount department stores for $2–5 each. Encourage each student to buy a flag for his or her bike, or provide the flags when kids show up for each ride. Quick-release axles make the flags easy to attach and detach.

Many students initially resist riding with these flags because they associate them with children's bikes. Admittedly, most serious adult bikers don't use flags. Still, the flag requirement is valid. The flag gives drivers earlier visibility of the bikers. Drivers moving at the speed limit will see your bikers three to five seconds earlier. That gives them additional time to adjust to your presence on the road by slowing down or giving you more space.

You can't make students ride with flags on their own personal time. You may not even want to use one yourself during your personal riding. However, riding with a group sponsored by the church or youth organization and under your responsibility is a different matter. Provide the best possible safety. It may be the protection you need on the road or in a court room. When everyone in the group is required to use a flag and knows the leader is firm about it, the resistance usually disappears.

3. *Bicycle inspection* should be required before any trip. Ask an experienced bike mechanic to help check each bike. Not only

will you be able to correct problems that will help the bikes run smoother and easier, but you can check essential safety items such as condition of tires and brakes. Students can also be counseled about the quality and condition of their bike (i.e., weight, gearing, etc.) in light of the trip they are planning to make with the group.

4. Safety Standards for your biking group should be printed and available for distribution to bikers and parents prior to the trip. Use the printed information as a basis for a verbal instruction about biking standards and practices for your group. Don't skip your safety standards orientation if on any day a new student joins your group to ride. Don't assume that the student knows how to ride safely. Protect yourself and everyone in the group (including the new student) with your safety orientation. Someday you may be asked by a lawyer to describe what safety instructions you gave to a student who was injured while biking under your supervision. Fight the temptation to take shortcuts in safety training. Remember to get this safety information to the parents prior to the trip.

5. Training Rides are essential to prepare students for the trip. Instructions on how to shift gears must be reviewed. If the trip planned will be through hilly or mountainous regions and the students live in a flat area, training needs to be strenuous and creative to prepare them for what they will face. Set a minimum number of miles a student should ride prior to the trip. Be sure to enforce strictly the safety rules on training rides.

6. Selecting the Route of the trip is best accomplished by sending out a scout team to drive several possible trips. The scouts should record in a notebook all the road conditions, directions, and places of interest where bikers would stop during a riding day. Check specific state maps for recommendations about what roads are best for biking. Often the state transportation department can supply that information. They will warn you about narrow roads with high-speed and truck traffic. Use the scout's notes to prepare a printed sheet of directions outlining each day's route. Written warnings can be given about dangerous sections of highway. The sheet can also list information about emergency phone numbers, medical facilities and the day's destination (with phone number).

Biking Safety Standards

- Make safety your primary concern—for you and for the members of your group. Obey all traffic rules just as you would driving a car. Ride single file just to the right of the solid white line.

- Communicate with the riders in your group. Group riding is different from riding alone. Riding behind another bike blocks your vision of the approaching road conditions. Use a "call system" to inform each other of any obstacles, safety hazards, turning, braking, or stopping. The lead rider calls out the message. Each rider should repeat the call until it is passed back to the last rider in the group. The last rider calls out any messages about approaching traffic so riders can maintain their safe, single file formation as cars and trucks pass by. The call system is vital to avoid accidents, flat tires, and bent rims.

- Be ready for dangerous road conditions. Avoid riding over potholes, large cracks, and grooves in the road. Any of these can cause a biker to lose his or her balance.

- In wet weather be aware of the additional time it takes for braking. Rain and water off the tires also impairs vision. Slow down and put more space between the bikes.

- Constantly watch for changes in road conditions. Call out broken glass, sand, gravel, dead animals, and all debris in the road.

- Bikes don't handle well on steel grated bridges (wet or dry). Slow down and ride cautiously.

- When in heavy traffic, anticipate any hazard that could occur in a split second (such as a person in a parked car opening a door).

- Watch speed when going downhill. Spread out and put more space between bikes. Allow more time to stop. Watch for traffic lights and stop signs at the bottom of hills. Warn everyone riding behind you.

Never Overlap Wheels. Overlapping is the greatest cause of serious accidents in group biking. Leaders must be relentless enforcing this rule. Overlapping is when the front wheel of one bike is parallel (side-by-side) with any portion of the rear wheel of the bike in front of it. In this situation the wheels are so close together that any movement side to side by either bike can cause the wheels to touch. Even the slightest brush of wheels can cause a rider (usually the rider following) to lose balance and become involved in an accident. Always keep a distance of at least two feet between the back tire of the lead bike and the front tire of the following bike. This distance must be increased in hazardous conditions such as steep down hills and wet roads. Riders must consistently and loudly call out braking and stopping situations to prevent bikers following from overlapping.

Ride as a Group. Stay together as a group in all circumstances. Find a pace that everyone can keep. Don't let the group be separated by large gaps of space. Make all turns or lane changes as a group. Move like a caterpillar with the lead rider and rear rider checking the approaching traffic and calling out directions. Use hand signals to warn vehicles of your intentions. No one should be turning or changing lanes apart from the group. Move through traffic lights and intersections together as a group as well. The senior leader in a group is best

CRACKED HEADS

Requiring bicycle helmets isn't much of a controversy today. I remember the day I changed my mind. Having ridden so many years and miles without a helmet, wearing one seemed unnecessary to me.

On this memorable day approximately one-third of our 50 riders were wearing helmets. We were cruising down a hill on a wide paved shoulder of the road into a small Connecticut town. Suddenly a car lurched out of the parking lot of a shopping center and stopped on the shoulder to check for oncoming traffic. The young driver didn't see us just 30 feet away and moving 22 to 24 miles per hour down the hill.

Brian, a 16-year-old on his first bike trip, was leading the group. He had no chance to stop his bike. When he hit the side of the car, the bike frame folded up like an accordion. Brian flipped over the front hood of the car and landed head first on the pavement. But the impact cracked open his helmet, not his head. Brian got up off the pavement scraped, bruised, scared . . . and alive.

That was the last year not wearing helmets was voluntary. Some situations are absolutely unavoidable. If you are going to ride a bike on the road, you will encounter those unavoidable situations when a helmet could mean the difference between life and death.

positioned in the last spot of the line where he or she can see the entire biking group. An additional leader can take one of the first three positions in the line.

Allow No Stupid Moves. What may seem safe when you bike individually is not safe for group riding. No riding without hands on the handlebars. No drafting other vehicles. No weaving as you ride. No squirting water bottles at others, especially toward groups who are passing. The natural response of the biker is to swerve left away from the water and into the traffic. Don't allow riders to wear headphones. Their hearing is key to their safety.

Get off the Road. When you stop for repairs, directions, food, or even an accident, it is important to immediately get off the road. Every bike and rider should be as far onto the shoulder of the road as possible. If you stop where there is little or no shoulder, move to another spot where riders can safely wait off the road while the problem is addressed.

Severe weather is another reason to get the bike group off the road entirely. Fog, heavy rain, and lightning require a decision by the group leader. Think about the ability of drivers moving at highway speed being able to see the group and avoid striking any of the bikers. Be cautious and get off the road immediately until the weather conditions improve.

Never ride in darkness. No group should be biking before sunrise or after sunset. Leaders should take note of sunset times and pull their groups off the road if they have not reached their destination. Take no chances in dusk light. Alternate transportation can be arranged. Be sure you have the phone number of where your group is staying so you can call for assistance.

Get off the road when the traffic conditions, the condition of the road, or a combination of the two factors give you reason to believe that a biker might fall into traffic or be hit by a vehicle. No cyclist likes to walk his bike; but on a bad road, walking beats riding in an ambulance or a hearse. The leader cannot be afraid to make this decision (no matter how unpopular) and stick with it.

Signs of Trouble

When is it unsafe for a student to ride? A well trained leader can recognize trouble by carefully observing the student bikers under his or her supervision. Here's a partial list of potentially dangerous situations:

1. Fatigue. Everybody gets tired on a bicycle trip; it's the leader's responsibility to monitor that fatigue and provide appropriate rest. When heads are consistently down and riders seem less alert, they are becoming tired. Fatigue makes bikers prime candidates for an accident. If students are not in good physical condition for the trip, arrange for them to ride only a portion of the day until they increase their strength. Fatigue is also the product of not getting enough sleep. Failure to enforce a curfew or allow enough sleep at night can lead to accidents on the road during the day. The longer the trip (in miles or days), the greater the possibility of accumulated fatigue affecting the group.

2. Faintness/Dizziness/Drowsiness. This is a threat to a rider's balance and ability to react. Leaders need to remind riders to speak up when they are experiencing these symptoms. Hot days, bright sun, upset stomachs, dehydration, and medication can cause these symptoms. Encourage students to speak openly about how they feel. Ask them directly if they feel any symptoms. Respond immediately by getting the students off the road and putting them into your support vehicle. Be careful of students using any medication during the day that causes drowsiness.

3. Dehydration and Heat Problems. Riders should drink regularly while cycling to replace fluids. Every bike should carry one or two water bottles filled with water or a sports exercise drink containing electrolyte supplements from which riders should take a drink every five or ten minutes. Don't wait to feel thirsty to begin drinking. The leader should remind students to drink as they ride. A reliable guide for detecting dehydration is the inability to urinate at least every two hours when actively exercising. When they cannot urinate, their body is holding on to fluids. This condition is easier to prevent than correct. Teach students this warning sign of dehydration and encourage them to speak up about how they feel.

Heat exhaustion is caused by the body's loss of important fluids and salt. The signs and symptoms are dizziness, pale skin, nausea, and rapid heartbeat. Treat such victims by removing them from the heat source, sponging them down with water, and giving them sips of fluid fortified with an electrolyte supplement or salt. Be careful in the cooling process not to send them into hypothermia.

Heat stroke is far more dangerous and comes on much more suddenly. Common symptoms are confusion, irrational behavior, rapid pulse and breathing, hot and dry skin, and loss of consciousness. To treat this condition, remove some clothing and moisten the body with cool water. Again, do not cool the body into a hypothermic state. Evacuation to a hospital is necessary.

4. Hyperventilation. When riders are climbing long hills, inhaling and exhaling heavily, they can develop a shallow breathing pattern that does not provide enough oxygen to their system. The faster they breath, the less oxygen they get into their system. They often panic, feeling a form of suffocation as they gasp for air. The leader must get such persons off the bike and seated in a safe spot with their heads down between their knees. In ideal circumstances, the leader should put a paper bag over the victim's nose and mouth and instruct them to breath deeply and slowly. Lacking a paper bag, an inventive leader can use a bandana or a shirt tent-style or even cup his hands over the student's nose and mouth. The victim needs more carbon dioxide in his or her lungs to restore normal breathing. Have the victim rest until the breathing returns to normal and the person feels confident enough to get back on the bicycle.

5. Sunburn. Moving through the wind, riders may not realize the burn that the sun is putting on their skin. In addition to the normal spots that you expect to be sunburned, special care should be given to protect the front of the upper legs, the back of the lower legs, and the ears, nose, and face. Long hours on the bicycle can numb a person to the power of the sun. Use generous amounts of sunscreen and sun block. Treat burns with aloe vera gel. Do not break blisters for fear of infection. Keep the affected area clean.

Who Carries the Gear?

The purists of bicycle touring carry all their gear on their bikes in panniers, a set of luggage packs over the wheels. While transporting everything under your own power gives a great feeling of self sufficiency , the packs make the bike much heavier and harder to maneuver. If you have younger, inexperienced riders, it is wiser and safer to supply a support vehicle (van or small truck) to carry their duffel bags and sleeping bags.

The support vehicle also plays a crucial safety role. It monitors the riding groups by moving along the route in a leap frog pattern—moving ahead and waiting on the side of the road for groups to pass by. If the vehicle is clearly marked with a sign or an orange flag, it alerts motorists to the presence of bikes on the road and attracts anyone who has helpful information for the group leaders. The support vehicle is available to take aboard any biker who is injured or sick. It gives the bike group leaders an immediate response to anyone who needs medical attention for any reason.

Mountain Biking

The popularity of mountain bikes opens additional cycling opportunities. The wider width tires give a rider more stability and confidence on the road. The ruggedness of the frame and tires enable a biker to ride through rough road conditions without having to swerve left into the road or risk falling. Mountain bikes are very appropriate for younger, less experienced riders.

Helmets should still be required on all roads and trails.

Mountain bikes have also opened up new trip possibilities. In many areas old railroad beds are being renovated for bike paths. Mountain bike trails offer trip opportunities off the paved road and away from the traffic. Many ski areas are now using their trails in summer for mountain biking. The advantage of such a trip is obvious—the traffic risk is removed. The disadvantage is the distance from civilization when medical help is required. The safety concerns of a mountain-biking trip should be treated like a backpacking trip on wheels.

Backpacking and Hiking

The storm came over the campsite with incredible speed. The young people were just crawling into their tents for the sleep they so desired after a long strenuous day. Several tents were pitched around the base of a tree.

Suddenly before a drop of rain had fallen lightning hit the tree. The crack of thunder shook the entire camp. The silence following the thunder was pierced by the hysterical crying of two girls from a tent near the tree.

Al, the youth group leader, had no idea what he would see when he looked inside the tent. One girl lay in her sleeping bag paralyzed. The zipper of the sleeping bag had melted and was permanently welded together. Part of the metal zipper was attached to the skin of this girl's leg. The other girl lay beside her, stunned and unable to hear.

The tent had been pitched within five feet of the tree that was struck by lightning. The roots of the tree extended out from the base and ran directly under the tent. The electrical current had traveled through the roots and into the tent.

One of the volunteer leaders helping with the trip was a surgeon. He assessed their situation and sent a leader for medical help. Fortunately Al and his crew were sleeping overnight near a campground just off the hiking trail. Within an hour the young women were on their way to the hospital.

The girls suffered minor burns from the lightning. The paralysis only lasted for 30 minutes. They were released from the hospital that evening into the care of their parents. Al had called the parents from the hospital. He said it was the most frightening talk he had ever had with a parent on the phone.

The awesome power of natural forces is always on display when a youth group hikes into the wilderness. When the power show becomes too intense, youth workers are often isolated from civilization and professional medical assistance. Al and his group were fortunate to be camped near civilization on that memorable evening. They were thankful to have a trained medical resource with them.

Hiking and backpacking can be very safe, but the smallest problem can become major when medical assistance is hours away. Natural forces and wilderness locations are not to be underestimated as risks for the safety of youth groups.

Hiking and backpacking are not simply camping. If a youth group wants a natural setting with some modern conveniences, a campground is the best choice, for it provides access to transportation and phones. Overnight hiking and backpacking trips that take groups into the wilderness and away from civilization require properly trained leaders.

Before You Hike: Leader Preparation
Before taking a group into the wilderness, the leader has some important work to do:
• Plan the trip with a high quality map noting any helpful information.
• Arrange enough leaders to provide a 1:3 adult-to-student ratio. (Ten students with three leaders is a maximum number for a wilderness experience.) Don't overlook parents as potential staff leaders. Provide a male staff member to travel with the female staff on an all-female trips to discourage aggressive and obnoxious male campers whom they might encounter.
• Find a trained medical professional (i.e., registered nurse or an emergency medical technician) to travel with you. At the very least, one of your leaders needs extensive first-aid training and experience.
• Take the trip yourself with your team of leaders prior to the group's hike.
• Talk with the other leaders about the potential dangers of the trip and work through some worst-case scenarios with them.

- Obtain and distribute information about contacting park rangers and local hospitals.
- Know the route of the trip so well that you know where and how to find emergency help.
- Invest in a two-way radio or borrow a cellular phone for the trip and set up a contacting schedule with your support team. Make several trial runs with the system to make sure you can contact them satisfactorily.
- Prepare a list of the names of your hikers, complete with medical and insurance information, to carry with you during the trip.
- Prepare a map and route of your trip plans with a contact person who can alert authorities if you experience difficulties.
- Pack a fully stocked first-aid kit. (see chapter 10 for suggestions on contents)

Ted and several students from his youth group woke up in the mountains of Pennsylvania to find their campsite covered with fresh snow—the product of a surprise spring storm. They weren't prepared for either the knee-deep snow or the windy, cold weather.

They were six miles from yesterday's drop off spot and a full two-day hike from the spot where their prearranged pick up would be waiting for them. How would they survive these days without suffering frostbite or exposure?

Fortunately Ted and his crew were in the hands of a capable guide they had hired to lead this trip. Two hours of difficult hiking through the snow brought them to a paved road and a waiting van. The guide had responded to the surprise weather conditions by using his portable radio to call his support team and arrange the rendezvous. He explained later that he always has alternate plans ready in case an emergency evacuation is ever needed. What could have been a tragic disaster for Ted and his students was averted by thorough and careful planning.

Student Preparation
Establish some standards of readiness to determine if a student is qualified to participate on a wilderness trip. Students should

experience some short, single overnight trips before they are accepted for a multiple-day trip that will take them far from civilization. The short trips will provide a clear picture of their physical fitness and emotional stability necessary for a longer, more challenging trip.

The most crucial piece of equipment on a hiking trip is a good pair of boots or shoes. They must be properly fitted and comfortable to avoid painful and crippling blisters. Students should wear them regularly prior to the trip.

Any equipment a student is required to furnish should be checked prior to the trip for its quality and reliability. Each student's backpack should be inspected and packed with a staff leader present to insure that the proper items are included and unnecessary items are left at home. If there is any reason to suspect that students are attempting to smuggle alcohol or drugs on the trip, pack the bag two days prior to the trip. The leader can store the fully packed bag under his or her supervision and release them when they arrive at the drop-off spot.

On the Trail

As you enter the woods and begin to hike the trail, be sure to sign in at the box provided by the forest ranger. This paper is not the place for jokes or phony information. Respect and use this safety procedure. Obey the laws and regulations of the park where you hike. Take time to familiarize your group with the rules and demand their compliance. Other than pocket knives, small axes, and saws, no one should be carrying any type of weapon (firearm, machete, etc.).

Never camp:

• Under tall trees that could attract lightning or whose branches or limbs could fall during a wind storm. Woodsmen call such trees widow makers.

• In tall dry grass. A fire could ignite and spread rapidly to engulf the tents.

• In a gully or a canyon. A flash flood could start several miles away and rush down, wiping out everything in its path.

• Near or below the high tide line on a beach or the shoreline.

• Under an overhanging cliff or bluff. A rock slide or avalanche could bury your campsite.

• Over top of roots of large tall tree (remember Al's lesson). Electrical current from lightning hitting the tree can travel through the root system and burn anyone or anything it contacts.

Water Purification. This is a necessary task, regardless of the water's source. Your first experience with vomiting and diarrhea caused by impure water will convince you. Purification can be accomplished by three methods—boiling, filtering, or chemical treatment. The chemical treatment is quicker than boiling and more reliable than filtering.

Cleaning Dishes and Utensils. Campers can come down with diarrhea as a result of dishes that have not be thoroughly cleaned or have not been sufficiently rinsed to remove all soap. Diarrhea is not only inconvenient and uncomfortable; it can trigger severe dehydration.

Food in the Camp. Never store food (even the smallest quantities) in the tents where campers are sleeping. Animals of all sizes and types will find a way into that tent perhaps with tragic results. Most obvious is the danger of bears who could do severe damage to any occupant. In bear-free areas, caution still must be taken to discourage common visitors like porcupines and raccoons. A night time encounter in close quarters with either of these animals could cause injuries. All food should be placed in a special food bag or backpack and hoisted up on to the limb of a tree where it cannot be reached from the ground or by climbing the tree. Take extra care to insure that students don't ignore your warning and take snacks to bed with them. The scent of food, even in the crumbs and the opened wrappers, is enough to attract some unwanted visitors.

Fire. Almost every young person loves to build a fire and play with it. The fire must be supervised by a leader at all times.

Ignore the pleading of the students and keep the fire small. Build it in an open area (no overhanging trees), in a pit, or inside a ring of rocks to protect it from spreading. Never use rocks from a lake or stream. They may explode when heated. Make sure the fire is safely away from any tents or tarps. Before you leave the campsite, extinguish the fire completely. Water down any partially burned logs that might ignite after you leave.

Hiking in Dense Underbrush. Watch for branches and brush swinging into the face and eyes of hikers following the person in front of them. Teach young people how to protect the person who is walking behind them. Never walk on or stand on loose rocks or logs when you can step over or around them. Falling can cause severe sprains or fractures that will seriously alter the outcome of the trip.

Group-mindedness. Hiking and backpacking with a youth group is not an individual experience. Every decision is a group decision. No student should be out of sight of a staff member when on the trail. No one should venture out of the camp area without a partner and giving notice to the leader.

Lost. The group needs prior instruction to know the international distress signal. The SOS signal is three repeated sounds (whistles, etc.) or flashes (flashlight or mirror). The rescue group is to respond with two repeated sounds or flashes. It is good preparation to carry a whistle in your pack at all times. Teach young people to only use the signal in the event of an actual need for help.

Hypothermia. When a person's body becomes unable to generate enough warmth to compensate for heat loss, he or she becomes a victim of hypothermia. It is easier to prevent than to treat. Hypothermia can be prevented by dressing appropriately for the weather, keeping the body and clothing dry, covering the head, neck, and hands, and wearing clothes that maintain insulating properties even when wet. Wet clothing or a cold wind on a body wet with perspiration can lead to hypothermia.

There are two stages of hypothermia. A mildly hypothermic person will complain of cold and have difficulty performing simple motor functions. They may become apathetic, perhaps shivering, and have a body core temperature as low as 95 degrees Fahrenheit. Move the person from the cold into a warm environment, then remove damp clothing or add warm insulation. Offer warm liquids and food.

The victim of moderate or severe hypothermia will exhibit slurred speech, stumbling, unresponsiveness, decreased pulse, and breathing difficulty. Body temperature will be below 95 degrees Fahrenheit. Cover the victim immediately. Do not allow the person to walk or move. Handle him or her gently. Get medical help. In all situations of potential hypothermia, respond to the signs and symptoms, even if the victim doesn't.

Frostbite. Frostbite is caused by the restriction or stoppage of blood circulation to the extremities such as fingers and toes. The loss of circulation allows the fluid in the tissues to freeze when the surrounding temperature is below 32 degrees Fahrenheit. Primary first aid for frostbite involves preventing additional freezing and further damage to the frozen tissue from thawing and re-freezing. The main symptom is white skin that is waxy and hard to the touch. The area may feel intensely cold and numb. Give the victim plenty of fluids. Rewarm the part only if it is not going to bear weight and will not refreeze. Do not rub or massage the area. Take the person to a hospital.

Insect Bites and Stings. Unless the victim suffers an allergic reaction, bites and stings are usually more painful than serious. For bee stings use a knife edge to scrape out the stinger. Using tweezers or grabbing the stinger with fingernails may squeeze more venom in the sting area. Wash with soap and apply a anti-sting lotion. If the victim suffers an allergic reaction, give him or her an antihistamine, keep calm, maintain the airway, and transport the person to a hospital. People who know they are allergic should carry an Ana-Kit that contains a premeasured injection to fight the reaction.

Poison Oak, Poison Ivy, and Poison Sumac. Learn to identify poisonous plants. Poison oak and poison ivy both go by the rule "leaves of three, let them be." The plants secrete a noxious oil that severely irritates the skin when transmitted by direct contact and contact with contaminated clothing. Signs appear within one or two days after contact: skin burns, itches, and sometimes blisters. If you suspect contact with such plants, remove the contaminated clothes and wash separately. Wash the skin with strong laundry soap and warm (not hot) water. Wipe down the affected area with rubbing alcohol. If rash develops, avoid scratching, for it could lead to a secondary infection if the blisters are opened. Apply cold compresses and a lotion containing hydrocortisone.

Rock Climbing and Rappelling

If you can't hire or recruit a certified experienced instructor, you and your youth group shouldn't even attempt rock climbing or rappelling. Most insurance companies will no longer cover these activities. Check your insurance policy.

If you go looking for a guide, ask about his or her training (National Outdoor Leadership School [NOLS] is probably the best) and the experience he or she has had leading groups. Check their references; don't take any shortcuts. The lives of your students will be in their hands. Be sure to take the staff on a pre-trip experience with the guide to get a clear understanding of what is involved.

Despite the best training and equipment, rock climbing and rappelling accidents do happen. Recently a youth organization suffered a fatality when the professional guide did not tie the rope to the harness correctly. It was something he had done successfully thousands of times prior. In this type of activity a small, rare mistake can mean severe injury or death.

ON THE WITNESS STAND

I can still hear Chrissy screaming. She was 30 feet below me hanging on a rope by her hair (literally). Chrissy was one of 15 students who had accepted the challenge from me and one of my volunteers to rappel down a 70-foot cliff. Charlie made his living as an arborist (tree trimmer) and climbed with ropes regularly. He had the equipment, the know-how, and the persuasiveness to talk me into offering this adventure to the kids at our YFC camp.

It had been a great afternoon until Chrissy's long hair came out of her bandana and became entwined in the rope. She was not wearing any protective head gear (a major blunder on my part). When her hair caught in the rope she panicked and abandoned her rappelling hand grip position to grab the rope any way she could to keep her hair from being pulled out of her head.

Charlie heard the scream and jumped over the edge Indiana Jones-style, grabbing an adjacent rope on the way down. It was extremely reckless, but effective. He reached Chrissy, stabilized her position, and cut her hair from the rope with his hunting knife. Slowly he lowered himself (Chrissy clung to him with a death hold) to safety.

We laughed and bragged about the whole incident later that night at our camp. It did give me a great opportunity to talk to Chrissy (a vocal agnostic) about who she was praying to while hanging on the rope. But I was a stupid, foolish leader who just dodged a major bullet. Except for Charlie's heroic reaction, Chrissy had been seconds from a major injury or death.

In a court of law I would have been asked about Charlie's credentials and training to lead such an activity. Why didn't we use protective head gear? Why didn't her parents know when she went to camp with us she would be repelling down a 70-foot cliff? The questions would be endless. The conclusion would be clear. I foolishly miscalculated the risk and allowed Chrissy to be in the situation that threatened her life.

CHAPTER NINE
Most Accidents Happen at Home

It was Friday night and time for "Death Tag!" With all the lights off in the church, the students hid throughout the building. The youth director searched for them, armed with butterscotch candies that he threw at them to "kill" them. In past games one student hid in the rafters above a false ceiling. During the game he slipped off the rafters and crashed through the ceiling to the floor. This night a young man fleeing through the basement ran into a water pipe and burst the pipe. Try explaining that to a trustee of the church.

Most of us in youth ministry acknowledge the need for safety when we are climbing a mountain or canoeing on a white water river. When the setting changes to our church building and our regular weekly meetings, we feel much more relaxed and complacent on safety issues. The scenery is so familiar that we are blinded to the hazards and risks. Like the mature, experienced water ski instructor who broke his own safety rules (see chapter 7), our familiarity with normal youth group activities breeds contempt for awareness of danger.

In chapter 2 we surveyed a church facility open for an evening of unstructured recreation and listed the potential dangerous situations. Most of us have learned to feel comfortable with how our youth ministry operates. It may look potentially hazardous to a newcomer, but we have adjusted our nerves to accept the risk. Most likely we have done these activities numerous times and operated with our loose rules without any serious injuries or problems.

The warning of this book calls youth leaders to recognize a changing culture that will examine and evaluate their activities and safety practices with greater scrutiny. What may have been quickly forgiven in the past may be cause for a lawsuit in the present and coming days.

Facility Hazards

Safety agencies tell us most accidents happen at home. If that is true, the regular meeting place of our youth group is the "home" location we should be safety-proofing. Often it is so familiar to us that we cannot see the hazards right in front of us each week.

- Are there smoke detectors and fire extinguishers in the building? Are the extinguishers hidden to keep our youth group kids from fooling with them? Without looking, do you know where they are? Is there fire emergency equipment in the kitchen?

- Are emergency phone numbers posted in a public place near the phone? Is there a phone to use in an emergency, or are they all behind locked doors?

- What access do our students have to balconies and high places in the church or building? Can they get onto the roof or out on the fire escape? Falls are a common reason for serious accidents and injuries.

- Is the recreation room or gym equipped with safety equipment like protective mats at the ends of the basketball court?

- Is there a well-stocked first-aid kit available?

Eyes on the Equipment

The greatest risk of danger with equipment isn't when the whole group is using it, but rather when it sits unsupervised. A careful youth leader keeps equipment and props under careful control and put away when not being used properly.

In Chapter 6, I recounted the story of a youth ministry

volunteer who was paralyzed by falling off the top of the cage ball at a field event. Just days ago, I was at a youth event where a six-foot cage ball was used for a great junior high game. Later in the evening, while most everyone was in an adjacent room eating snacks, I walked into the game room to discover an eighth grader who had hopped on top of the ball and was starting to walk on it, to the amazement of his two watching friends. I spoke softly and calmly so I wouldn't frighten him into falling. When he was safely on the ground and out the door, I shook my head in disbelief at how easy it is to leave temptation in their way.

One youth group leader hooked up a rope swing from the cathedral ceiling in their youth room meeting area. He had one of the volunteer leaders swing on the rope as part of a skit they did for the kids in the meeting. After the meeting the rope was still hanging from the ceiling hook, but it was not attached securely. A young man tried to mimic what he had seem the leader do during the meeting. He grabbed the rope, swung off the 10-foot ledge, and immediately crashed to the floor. It was a big surprise for him. Fortunately he walked away with just some bruises.

Teen Vehicles

This is a hot home safety issue. Youth leaders can't control what teens drive to their meetings. You probably have cars, trucks, motorcycles, mopeds, and bicycles of many types in your parking lot. That parking lot can be a dangerous spot for your kids.

Teenagers have always been able to find something exciting (and dangerous) to do with motorized vehicles. Last summer one group had a lot of fun "surfing the hood" of the cars. Several students would stand on the front hood of the car surfer-style as the driver whipped around the parking lot. The driver would accelerate and brake, trying to make the surfers lose their balance. Our family was asked to pray for one young man who was in a coma after he lost his footing on the hood and hit his head on the pavement.

A youth leader can't wipe out the fascination teenagers have with motorized vehicles. These games will come and go. But in the course of these games students will be hurt. Our responsibility is to monitor what goes on when they are under our supervision and demand their best behavior and safe operation of those vehicles. For more on this subject see the discussion of teen drivers in chapter 5.

Dangerous Games

Food Games. Campus Life calls it Chubby Bunnies. You may have a different name for it. You get a student to fill his or her mouth with marshmallows, grapes, etc., one at a time, while repeating a phrase like "chubby bunnies." Several students are in competition to see who can have the most items in their mouth while still being able to repeat the phrase. It is very funny to hear students slurring their response while slobbery food drips out of their mouths. Can you recognize the danger? Gasping for breath, a piece of food could be drawn into their wind pipe, causing them to choke.

This game practically begs you to perform the Heimlich Maneuver on a participant. I can hear the groaning from my YFC friends—"But it is so funny. . . . I've never seen anyone choke." I hear your objections, but think about it. Is it worth the risk? The comic value of the game would be lost in a court room when you are asked to explain the purpose of the game.

We should give special scrutiny to any forced-feeding game that puts large amounts of food in a person's mouth. Dropping food into the mouth of person lying on the floor or shooting food into a person's mouth is also not a good idea because of the risk of choking. We used to hold pizza eating contests where guys would eat a triangular slice in less than 10 seconds. It can't be healthy or safe for young people to ingest large amounts of food without chewing. Should we as leaders be encouraging the game and challenging them to go faster?

Move the Furniture, Fred. Lack of foresight and preparation can put a dent in the head of a student. If you conduct a game in a living room setting be sure to allow adequate space for a person to fall, or place spotters around the room so students cannot fall.

A young man fainted during a game in a family room. He was blowing on one end of a clear plastic tube trying to force a raw egg (in the middle of the tube) into the mouth of the student who was blowing into the other end. When his breath was exhausted, he fainted and fell backward into the corner of a table. The impact split open his head. It meant a trip to the emergency room and stitches to close the wound.

A young lady was placed in the center of the circle for a game called Pass the Bod. She was instructed to stand stiff while the other students sat in a circle around her with their stocking feet against her legs. When she crossed her arms in front of her chest she was to lean toward the group. The students on the floor were supposed to push and pass her around the group. Usually this game is a blast, but on this night when the young lady was pushed toward the other side of the circle the students didn't catch her. She landed face first on the edge of a wooden end table, knocking out her two front teeth.

In both of these accidents, the leaders had not provided spotters to guard the participants if they should fall. Pass the Bod needs several reliable spotters around the circle. The games were played in inappropriate settings. The close proximity of the furniture reflects a lack of planning and anticipation of what could happen when people fall. Games need to be selected according to the physical setting of the meeting room.

Throwing Games. Throwing any objects in a youth group meeting needs to be carefully monitored. Throwing activities need to be defined with a safe target, specific objects to be thrown, and a clear starting and stopping point. If a "throwing" atmosphere develops in the meeting you can expect anything and everything to be thrown—paper wads, pencils, wrapped candy, etc. Some of the objects will be absolutely harmless. Others can be dangerous. You can't expect young people to always know the difference and to exercise good judgment.

Hitting Games. Who defines how hard students are supposed to hit a person in the head with a newspaper during a game? Most students may hit gently and harmlessly. A student, frustrated or excited about the game, might forget his strength and blast a younger, smaller group member in the head or face. Some students easily lose control when they are struck by someone with whom they might feel some competition. They might lose control and get out of hand to go "one up" on someone else in the group.

Beware the Eyes. Spraying anything in the eyes and face of a young person is strictly taboo. You might damage the eyes or a person's glasses or contact lenses. Sharp objects should not be used in games where a sudden unexpected movement might cause them to strike a person's eye. Watch for blindfold games where a person might unknowingly strike another person's eyes. I certainly felt different about my cops and robbers game (see chapter 6) when six hands started pawing my face and eyes trying to pull a piece of tape off my face.

No Weapons. We used to stage a fake assassination in youth group meetings to shock everyone and set the stage for discussing violence. A stranger (arranged by our staff) would walk into the meeting and fire a starter pistol. A staff leader would be "struck" Hollywood style and fall to the ground bleeding as the stranger escaped. Although it was a dramatic, that was probably not one of our better discussion starters. It was simply a stunt that pumped the emotions of kids. Today I would never do any stunt involving weapons in my meetings. Some young person sitting in the meeting might pull out a real weapon to avenge what he just witnessed without knowing it was just an act.

Hide-and-Seek Games. Youth leaders interviewed for this book told numerous stories about young people (and leaders) hurt during hide-and-seek games in their church buildings. The game encourages students to find remote and unlikely places in a building to hide. Students have gotten stuck in crawl spaces and fallen through ceilings. One young man fell through the ceiling into a storage room off the sanctuary and just missed being impaled on the large metal candelabra (used for weddings) being stored there.

Scaring Kids. Manny was new to the youth group. He liked coming with his friends. Everyone seemed to like him. One night the group set up a funny game where after spending a few minutes in the dark, a person would be blasted with a bright strobe light and see himself in a mirror. The game really worked well on Manny. When the light flashed and he saw a face right in front of him he reacted spontaneously and punched the mirror, cutting his hand. If you decide to scare teens, be ready for a physical reaction or response. Don't have anything or anyone within reach that could cause injury. Manny's family sued the church and was awarded $25,000 in damages.

Rough Games. Without protection, heavy contact games in the church gym or the yard outside are an unnecessary risk to the safety of the young people involved. Many youth groups love to have a friendly game of tackle football (leaders included). Neck, head, and dental injuries are the major risks. These injuries are much harder to repair than bruises or even broken bones. The most likely scenario for injury is when young people of varying physical sizes and abilities are in the same game. The weaker and less skilled are at high risk when they have no protection.

Sports Plus. When Terry showed up with a mini trampoline, everyone in the church gym lined up for the slam dunk contest. During the first night a staff leader wrecked his knee. Terry missed in his attempt to swing on the rim after his dunk and fell to the floor breaking both of his arms. With spotters and some supervision sports activities like this can be within the safety guidelines. Terry and his leader didn't take time to think about making it safe.

Outdoor Field Games. For a full listing on camps and retreats, see chapter 6.

Dangerous Topics

Suicide. A youth group meeting led by a young inexperienced staff leader tackled the topic of suicide. Someone asked if a person who was a Christian would go to heaven if he or she committed suicide. The discussion focused on how heaven would be so great because all the problems of life on earth would be forgotten. None of the leaders wanted to say that suicide victims go to hell because some of the students had a friend who had taken his life.

Several young people with many problems and struggles went home that night with the thought that the sooner they could get to heaven, the better it would be for them. During that week one of them made an unsuccessful suicide attempt.

A suicide discussion can provoke an interest in the exact behavior you are trying to condemn (the same is true for discussions of the occult). The youth leader faces a tough dilemma when the need arises to discuss the subject. It should never be scheduled into the meeting calendar routinely or handled casually. If it is necessary to discuss suicide, be sure to present a clear message that it is never a good answer to any problem a person is facing. Be alert to any young person who indicates any interest in the subject or is facing pressure or depression. Give them personal attention and follow up with further discussion immediately after the meeting, within 24 hours, and throughout the week.

Sexual or Physical Abuse. These topics are very hot and loaded with deep emotion. Extreme care must be taken not to trivialize the way you handle these matters. The chances are good that someone in your group has been abused. The youth leader should seek help to handle this subject carefully.

The safety factor is the liability leaders carry if they learn about abuse in the lives of students. This information should be handled with complete confidentiality in the context of the youth group. It will hurt young people to have a staff leader discuss confidential information with any other student. Information on reporting abuse can be found later in this chapter.

Sex. Today's youth culture is dominated by sexual topics and information. Josh McDowell's "Why Wait?" campaign reports that church teenagers are engaging in sexual activity at a rate similar to the general teenage population—approximately 60 percent. When sexuality is discussed in your youth ministry, leaders need to be very careful. In a large group setting both male and female staff can interact with the whole group. Small group discussions or one-to-one counseling, though, should be conducted strictly by the same gender staff leader. It is extremely dangerous and totally inappropriate for male leaders to be counseling teenage girls about their sexuality. The same principle applies to female staff and teenage boys.

Special Events
When you travel with your group to a one-night special event, think about how their safety can be protected. Transportation is a key issue. Have your staff prepared with information and directions so that no one gets lost or separated from the group. Don't let the excitement of arriving at your special destination cause the group to ignore simple safety practices like crossing the street in traffic. The daughter of a youth leader was running from a youth event to the church bus without regard to the traffic on the street. She was struck by a car and killed.

Beware of events with a general admission policy (no reserved seats). If there is a wait for the doors to open, the crowd can develop an aggressive attitude about getting the best seats. Pushing and shoving can lead to a mob scene when the doors open. It is illegal in many cities to have large events in concert hall/stadium settings with just general admission tickets. Don't allow your students to run into the hall to get their seats. If they fall, they could be trampled and seriously hurt. If you find yourself in a potentially dangerous situation at a concert or special event, don't be afraid to voice your concern to security guards or people in charge. You can speak up to the groups around you and ask for calm for the safety of everyone. If necessary, pull your group off to the side of the crowd until the situation is less dangerous.

Give specific instructions to your students about the conduct you expect from them at a concert or special event. Be sure they know their boundaries, where to find you, where and when to meet for departure, and not to leave the facility for any reason. Work out a procedure with your staff to check up on all your students during the evening. You don't need any surprises at the end of the night.

When you return to the church or your pick-up point, an adult should remain there until all the students have been picked up by parents or designated drivers. Try to stick to the arrival and departure times you set for parents. Have a phone chain set of parents whom you can call if you are going to be more than 30 minutes late. If you are taking students home and are delayed, stop to have the students call home. A worried, angry parent is tough to handle late at night. If the youth ministry staff is taking everyone home, have each driver confirm with you that everyone is home safely. That short phone call is a perfect time for you to say thanks for their help, while sending a message of concern for every young person and his or her family.

Discipline Problems

In the ideal world, youth group students listen to the leaders and carefully follow all their instructions. But do I need to remind you that we live in a fallen world? We all have days when our students seem uncontrollable and deaf to our guidance.

Young people running out of control are like an infectious disease in the atmosphere of the group. This attitude threatens the safety and well being of everyone involved. The youth leader needs to stop any out-of-control actions immediately before the problem spreads. Picture a table of students and leaders in a camp dining room. If two people at a single table start throwing food at each other, how long does it take to get other students and tables involved and throwing food. The responsible leader must never be afraid to step into any situation like that and gently but firmly remind the young people of the safety standards and who ultimately is in charge of the youth program.

Sometimes it is just silliness getting out of hand. I remember a fall weekend retreat when squirt guns advanced to cups of water that progressed to bowls, pitchers, and buckets of water.

I was in the kitchen working with the students who were on dishwashing duty. I was angered when some of them left their posts to join the water mania. I was also angered by the mess they made spilling water all over the kitchen floor.

When I had reached my boiling point, I grabbed one of the little guys who had hijacked the kitchen faucet and forcefully picked him up and threw him out the door onto the steps of the building. Everyone else got the message and scattered for cover. I physically hurt this young man. I was mad and had lost my temper. I had to publicly apologize to the whole group later that evening.

Youth leaders must not hit, punch, fight, or in any way physically abuse any student. It may prompt a legal action against you. Verbal abuse may be just as bad. Calling names and using sarcasm may win the initial battle, but these actions undermine the long-term ministry you will have with any group or individual.

When you are facing a young person who is physically acting out, hurting you or others, you must restrain them to protect the safety of others in the group. However the force of the youth leader must be defensive and restrained. Youth leaders can obtain special training in passive resistance, a satisfactory way of calming a person who is out of control. Check with a secular health and human service agency in your area for additional information on such training.

Safety Issues and Discipline

Are students leaving your meetings and activities early or disappearing for periods of time during the meeting? You can't erect a wall around your youth program to keep kids in, but you do have an obligation to the parents. Response to this behavior is somewhat related to the age of the young people, but anyone in junior high school or high school is still under the authority and supervision of their parent/guardian. If the parents think the kids are attending the youth group, the youth leader must tell them if in fact those kids are not.

When a young person exits early, the youth leader should confront that person directly and let him or her know the action is unacceptable. The leader should also outline the obligation he or she has to the parents. If the student continues to cut out, the youth leader must inform the parents and work together to change the behavior.

Drug Problems

How would you handle a strong suspicion by one of your volunteer leaders that a young person who is attending your group regularly is selling drugs to other youth in your group? What is your safety responsibility when you are providing the social meeting place for these transactions? Experience has taught me you can't turn your head and think the problem will go away. However, you shouldn't jump to conclusions and condemn the suspected person without a thorough investigation.

If kids want to sell and buy drugs, it is almost impossible for you to stop them from doing so, on or off your turf. However, you can take action. Confront each person suspected of being involved as a seller or buyer. They may lie to your face, but you can send a strong message about how you are going to fight the sale and use of drugs in the youth program. You can let them know that they will be under your watchful eye. Explain that you will personally confront them and bring other significant people (like their parents) into the matter if you have any evidence of their involvement. Then keep your promises. It's another way to show you care.

Have you decided what your response will be to students who show up to your meetings or activities showing signs of drinking or drug use? Will you let them stay and sit quietly in the meeting or will you ask them to leave? The youth ministry team needs to make that decision prior to the incident. If you do decide to let them stay, what special precautions will the youth ministry staff make to keep them from disrupting the meeting or hurting others?

The youth leader should not be handling these matters alone. Although it may seem embarrassing or condemning to your leadership, share these issues with your superior and/or board leaders. Don't let them be surprised about a drug problem in their ministry when some bad news becomes public. Ask for their help and guidance. They share the responsibility with you. When it is appropriate, talk to parents individually. They should not be left uninformed about major struggles in the life of their young person. Your pastor or director can be of great help to you as you relate to the parents.

Reporting Sexual Abuse and Physical Abuse

All suspicions of sexual abuse or physical abuse must be reported by volunteer workers to the head of the youth ministry. The head of the youth ministry should discuss these reports immediately with the director or pastor of the organization.

All this should be done quickly and confidentially.

In many states the professional youth worker or pastor has been designated a mandated reporter who must report any allegations of abuse to a hot line run by the state government.

Check the regulations of your state and comply with them. Often there is a mandated time period (24 to 48 hours) in which youth workers must report what they have learned. Learn the process and system in your state.

The first time I called the sexual abuse hot line, I agonized over my decision. One of our female volunteers had been told by a 16-year-old girl that her stepfather was coming into her room at night and sexually touching her. When the volunteer told me, I was shocked. This was an active church family. Everything about this family looked great on the outside.

We sent one of our female staff workers with the volunteer to talk with the girl to confirm what she had said. The staff worker then reported the girl's allegations to me. As the director of the program, I knew the law required me to make the call. I was afraid of what would happen to everyone involved and how the state agency would respond. I knew my call would set off a chain reaction that would forever alter the lives of these people.

I called the sexual abuse hotline. I was impressed with how much care and time the state agency took with my report and my concerns about the family. I realize that state agencies mishandle some situations and that the quality of the response depends on the person assigned to the case, but I found some good people waiting at the other end of the line to help. They responded immediately, contacting the young woman at school and the parents when they arrived home from work. The mother admitted that she had suspicions but had been afraid to confront her spouse. The stepfather agreed to undergo counseling. The young woman was taken out of the home and placed with her grandmother several miles away.

There are still many issues facing each person in that family, but our action brought about significant positive change in that young woman's life. She hated us for a few weeks after we reported it. That was hard on all of us, especially the volunteer whom she initially told. Several months later, though, she was grateful we had acted and that she was not being abused anymore.

Inappropriate Staff Relationships

One of the crucial safety issues of ministry each week from your home base is the relationship the youth ministry staff have with the young people in the program. In chapter 4, I discussed the standards for sexual conduct for youth ministry staff (paid and volunteer). These standards must be more than a piece of paper, signed and placed in a file. They must be followed each week by the staff and monitored regularly by the leader.

The story of Steve, a volunteer staff guy who had been accused of rape by a girl in the club (see chapter 4), reminds us that youth ministry today requires special precautions. Allegations of sexual misconduct in a youth ministry will destroy the credibility of God's work in that community. Special attention must be paid to the habits and practices of staff so that no actual misconduct can begin to grow or be alleged against any youth ministry staff person.

There should not be even the hint of any romantic or sexual attraction between staff and young people. Staff must be alert not to transmit any verbal or nonverbal messages that would suggest it. Dating or going out with any high school student should be absolutely forbidden to youth ministry staff and volunteers. Staff should use the buddy system (having another staff present or outside hearing distance but clearly visible) when talking privately or counseling a student of the opposite sex. Driving alone with students of the opposite sex should be avoided. Physical contact (touching, hugging, kissing, massaging, etc.) that might be interpreted as romantic or sexual should be prohibited between staff and students. Staff who seem to focus on one or two kids as favorites must be counseled to widen their approach or face dismissal from the ministry. Unfortunately, the safety of staff spending long periods of time alone with students (even of the same sex) is being questioned these days. Relational ministry is being redefined as having a third person along to verify our pure motives.

Any suspicions of misconduct or signs of romantic interests should be voiced and confronted immediately. Put a watch on people who continue to walk too close to the line. Those who have impure motives are often skilled at hiding the truth. Don't be naive or uninformed. Be active in maintaining upstanding relationships with all your students. Anyone who refuses to comply with your standards or who violates your written guidelines should be brought before your supervisor to discuss how changes will be made or how the person will be released from the youth ministry team.

CHAPTER TEN
Dealing with Problems and Injuries

As I reached the crest of the hill, I saw bikers standing in the road 300 yards ahead. Someone was lying along the edge of the road. I covered the distance in record time and jumped off my bike looking for the group's leader. The teenagers stood motionless like frozen statues. The screams came from our leader who was lying face down on the pavement in a growing pool of blood.

Stacy was a summer volunteer on our bike trip staff. She had gotten too much sun on the first day out of Montreal. This was her first day back on the bike after four days in the support van. I would learn later that she was riding real tight on the back wheel of the lead biker to conserve her strength. She touched that back tire and hit a rut in the road launching her over the handle bars. Her face skidded to a stop on the pavement.

Her screams signaled she was conscious and breathing. I barked out orders for two students to get to a phone at a house across the road. I described our location as they turned to run. Stacy began to cough and choke. She lifted her face from the pavement. I checked her airway. Surprisingly her teeth looked intact. As with any injury to the mouth or nose, the blood was flowing profusely. I called for the first aid kit and the gauze compresses to slow down the bleeding. There were more cuts on her body than we had pads of gauze.

167

Inside I was terrified. This was way over my head and the minimal first-aid training I had completed. I prayed and worried at the same time. What was I going to do if she lost consciousness or started having convulsions? We were 10 miles outside of the nearest town. How long would it take the ambulance to find us?

My prayers were answered when a woman stepped out of a car and announced she was an emergency room nurse. She pulled a sleeping bag out her trunk to keep Stacy warm. Until the ambulance arrived, she worked like an angel sent to help us.

It took 73 stitches to close the gashes in Stacy's face. Three months later you couldn't have guessed she had been lying on the side of that road. Though her scars disappeared quickly, my feeling of inadequate preparation for a medical emergency stayed with me. Everyone I know in youth ministry has a deep desire to help people who are in need. Each of us can learn how to respond to physical needs in these moments of emergency if we will take time to be trained and prepared.

First Aid

The following information does not substitute for certified first-aid training that should be required of all youth ministry staff. This section should not be regarded as a replacement for seeking immediate assistance from a trained medical professional or a medical facility.

This information is designed only to alert youth leaders to common problems and first-aid techniques that they should learn from a qualified trainer or organization. This information does not constitute training in first aid. Every youth ministry should have staff trained in first aid at all activities.

With that warning in mind, administering first aid is often just a matter of common sense. The primary task is to remain calm, assess the situation, call for help, provide comfort, and tend to the needs of the injured person as best you are able until help arrives. The basic principle of first aid is to do good if you can, while being careful not to do any harm.

Three Actions to Take in Any Emergency
1. Check the scene and the victim(s)
2. Call 911 or your local emergency number
3. Care for the victim(s)

Basic Steps of First Aid:

1. Upon seeing the injured person, assess the situation for any additional possibility of injury to any one else (including yourself). Make sure no one else will be injured. Would you be in danger if you tried to approach the victim to administer first aid? Don't put yourself in danger.

2. Do not move the injured person unless he or she is in an immediate, life-threatening situation. Anytime an injured person is moved there is risk of additional injury that might cause permanent damage or death. If you have to move the victim, do it as quickly and carefully as possible. Avoid twisting or bending the victim, who might have a neck or spine injury.

3. Call 911 or the local emergency number. If possible send another person present to make the call.

When You Know You Should Call 911
When the person:
- is or becomes unconscious.
- has trouble breathing.
- has chest pain or pressure.
- is bleeding severely.
- has pain or pressure in the abdomen that does not go away.
- is vomiting or passing blood.
- has seizures, severe headache, or slurred speech.
- appears to have been poisoned.
- has injuries to the head, neck, or back.
- has possible broken bones.

Calling 911: What to Tell Them
- the exact location or address of the emergency
- the telephone number from where you are calling
- your name
- what happened to injure the victim

- how many people are involved
- the condition of the victim(s)
- what first aid is being administered

Do not hang up until the dispatcher hangs up. He or she may need more information or may instruct you on how to care for the victim. Return to care for the victim until the ambulance arrives. If you send someone else to call, be sure that he or she knows the answers to these questions. Remind the caller not to hang up before the dispatcher does.

4. Begin caring for the victim. Always care for life-threatening situations before those that are not life-threatening. Watch for changes in the victim's breathing and consciousness. Keep the person warm. Help the victim rest comfortably. Calm and comfort the victim.

5. If the victim is unconscious you should check three signs:
- *Is the victim breathing?* If not, you have a life-threatening situation. Check by putting your face close to the person's mouth and nose. Watch to see if his or her chest rises or falls. Check the airways for blockage. If there is no breathing you must give the victim a couple breaths.
- *Does the victim have a pulse?* Place your finger on the front of the person's neck in the groove next to the Adam's apple. If there is a pulse but the person is not breathing, you will have to do rescue breathing. If there is no pulse, you will have to do cardiopulmonary resuscitation (CPR). At that moment you will be glad you sought training from the Red Cross or other organization. Don't wait until you are in this situation to recognize your need for training.
- *Is the victim bleeding severely?* Check the victim's body from head to toe for signs of bleeding. Bleeding is severe when it spurts out of a wound. Control the bleeding by placing a clean covering such as a sterile dressing over the wound and applying pressure. A dressing can be any clean cloth or absorbent material (clothing, bandana, or sanitary napkin). Add additional dressings to the wound while maintaining constant pres-

sure until the bleeding is controlled.

6. If the victim is conscious, ask him or her what happened. A verbal response confirms the victim's breathing and pulse. Look for any other life-threatening conditions. Talk to the victim or any witnesses to determine what care you need to give. Check the person for any problems. Don't move the victim or ask him or her to move. Watch for changes in breathing and consciousness. Look for a medical alert tag on the neck or wrist. If the injury or illness is related to the person's condition, call the number listed for help.

7. Stabilize any fractures or dislocations to prevent any further discomfort or harm. Any setting of a fracture or dislocation must be done by a trained medical professional.

8. Always treat for shock. Shock is a life-threatening condition even if the injury is not. Shock can be brought on by injury, poisoning, illness, allergic reaction, and even by seeing someone else injured. The signs and symptoms of shock are weakness, pale color, cool and clammy skin, irregular breathing, nausea, dizziness, and shivering. The first task is to maintain the injured person's body temperature by wrapping him or her in an emergency blanket, sleeping bag, or extra clothing if the outside temperature is cold. If the temperature is hot, keep the person cool by creating shade. Always try to keep the person insulated from the ground. The general rule is to keep the injured person lying down, comfortable and resting with the feet raised (except in case of head, neck, or back injury or if you suspect broken bones). Control any external bleeding. Calm and reassure the victim. Although the person is likely to be thirsty, don't give him or her anything to eat or drink. If the injured person feels like moving or sitting up, don't restrain him or her.

9. If the person has a partially blocked airway and is coughing forcefully, let him or her try to cough up the object. A person who can cough is getting enough air to breath. Stay with him and encourage him to keep coughing. If the victim can't dislodge the object, call an ambulance.

A person whose airway is completely blocked will not be able to speak, cough forcefully, or breathe. The victim may cough weakly or make high pitched noises. Have a bystander call an ambulance while you begin care. To open the airway quickly, give a series of quick hard thrusts to the victim's abdomen. Acquaint yourself thoroughly with the Heimlich maneuver.

Dealing with Common Injuries

Open Wounds (Cuts and Lacerations). The best treatment is cleansing the wound with antibacterial soap and water. Apply a clean, non-stick dressing and secure it with adhesive tape. For serious bleeding, apply direct pressure immediately using a clean dressing. If you don't think the wound also involves a broken bone, elevate the wound above the heart to slow the bleeding. When the bleeding stops, secure the wound with a compression bandage and travel to the hospital for additional treatment. If the bleeding cannot be controlled, put pressure on the nearby artery (pressure point). Treat for shock. It is brought on by a loss of blood or a disruption in the circulation system. Infection is a major concern for all wounds. Always clean with soap and water before applying an antibacterial ointment to prevent infection. After you have completed caring for the victim, be sure to wash your hands immediately.

Severe Wounds. If a part of the body has been severed or torn off, try to find the part and wrap it in sterile gauze or any clean material. Put the wrapped part in a plastic bag. Keep it cool with ice, but do not freeze it. Take it to the hospital with the victim. Doctors may be able to reattach it.

If an object is impaled in the wound of a victim, do not try to remove it. Place several dressings around it to keep it from moving. Bandage the dressings in place around the object.

Wounds that break through the abdomen can cause the organs to push out. Carefully remove clothing from around the wound. Cover the organs with a moist sterile or clean dressing and cover it with plastic wrap. Place a folded towel or other cloth over the dressing to keep the organs warm.

Dental. If the victim has had a tooth knocked out or damaged, place a sterile dressing directly in the space now vacant or damaged. Tell the victim to bite down carefully. If you can recover the tooth, it is important to get it replanted in the socket within an hour. Handle the knocked out tooth with care, picking it up by the chewing edge (crown) not the root. Do not touch the root part of the tooth. If possible place the tooth back into the socket. Bite down gently and hold the tooth in place with a sterile dressing. If it can't be placed back in the socket, place it in a container of cool, fresh milk until you reach the dentist. If no milk is available, use water.

Eyes. If any chemical or debris gets in a person's eye, flush the eye with large amounts of water. Be sure to flush from the inside corner of the eye (nearest to the bridge of the nose) outward so the other eye is not also contaminated. Continue to flush the eye for 10 to 15 minutes until you are sure the chemical or debris has been removed. Remove any thickened substance from the eye with a clean moist cloth. Flush the eye again. Do not put any medications in the eye. Cover the injured eye with a sterile gauze pad and take the person to the hospital immediately.

Burns. Minor burns usually don't require medical attention. Treatment, however, should be taken seriously. The affected part should be immersed in cool water to reduce pain and stop the burning sensation. Clean the area with soap and water and apply a topical anesthetic to reduce pain. For more severe burns that blister or have deep tissue damage, the victim needs immediate medical attention. Don't apply ice directly to any burn unless it is very minor. Don't touch a burn with anything except a clean covering. Don't remove pieces of cloth that stick to the burned area. Don't try to clean a severe burn. Don't break blisters or use any kind of ointment on a severe burn.

Sprains. Falls or hits that suddenly twist a joint can cause sprains to wrists, knees, and ankles. It is almost impossible to distinguish between a break and a sprain without an X-ray. You should assume that the limb is broken, then elevate it and immobilize it. Apply a cold pack to minimize swelling until the injured person can be examined at the hospital.

Spinal Injuries. Signs of spinal injury include a change in consciousness, problems with breathing and vision, inability to move a body part, ongoing headache, nausea, vomiting, and loss of balance. When you recognize these signs call an ambulance at once. While you wait for assistance give care by helping the victim minimize any movement of his or her head or spine. Place your hands on both sides of the victim's head. Position the head gently in line with the body and support it in that position until medical personnel arrive. If you feel resistance or it hurts the victim as you try to do this—stop. Support the head as you found it.

Seizures. These may range from mild blackouts that could be mistaken for daydreaming to sudden uncontrolled muscular contractions lasting several minutes. Stay calm, knowing that most seizures last only a few minutes. Have someone call for an ambulance. Protect the person from injury and keep his or her airway clear. Don't put *anything* in the person's mouth, though, especially your fingers. If there is fluid, saliva, blood, vomit in their mouth roll the person over on one side to drain it and keep the airway open.

Fainting. This is a temporary loss of consciousness. It is often preceded by paleness and perspiring. To care for fainting, place the victim on his or her back, elevate the feet and loosen any restrictive clothing. Although fainting victims recover quickly with no lasting effects, the symptom may actually be a signal of a more serious condition.

Asthma Attacks. Asthma is a condition that narrows the air passages and makes breathing very difficult. The asthma victim makes wheezing noises when trying to breathe. Attacks are triggered by an allergic reaction to food, medication, pollen, or insect stings. The attacks can also be brought on by physical activity or emotional distress. Asthma victims are usually armed with medication to control an attack. Young people should be carrying that medication with them, especially on a trip.

What About AIDS?

Will you be infected with AIDS if you give first aid to a person who is HIV positive? How do you know if a person is carrying the HIV virus when you are preparing to administer first aid?

AIDS stands for acquired immunodeficiency syndrome. It is caused by the human immunodeficiency virus (HIV). When the virus gets into the body, it damages the immune system that fights infection. The virus enters the body in three basic ways: 1) through direct contact with the bloodstream; 2) through the mucous membranes lining the eyes, mouth, throat, rectum, and vagina; and 3) through the womb, birth canal, or breast milk.

The virus cannot enter through the skin unless it is cut or broken at the point of contact. Even then, the possibility of infection is very low unless there is direct contact for a lengthy period of time. Saliva is not known to transmit HIV.

• The likelihood of HIV transmission during a first aid situation is very low. You are most likely to give first aid to someone you know. Always give care in ways that protect you and the victim from disease transmission.

• If possible, wash your hands before and after giving care, even if you wear gloves.

• Avoid touching or being splashed by another person's body fluids, especially blood.

• Avoid eating and drinking or touching your mouth, eyes, or nose while providing care, or before you wash your hands.

• Avoid touching objects that may have been contaminated with blood.

• Avoid handling any of your personal items such as combs or keys while providing care, or before washing your hands.

• Be prepared with a first-aid kit that includes waterless antiseptic hand cleaners and disposable gloves.

Stocking Your First-Aid Kit

Bandages, Dressings, and Other Items
- sterile gauze pads in a variety of two-by-two and four-by- four inch pads
- roller gauze: Kling or Kerflex
- non-adhering dressing: Telfa pads (coat with antibacterial ointment or petroleum, but change frequently to prevent drying out and adhering to the skin)
- one-inch adhesive tape
- butterfly bandages or steristrips assortment
- Ace™ Wrap: three-inch-wide bandage
- large compress: use feminine hygiene pads
- assortment of cloth bandages
- moleskin (for the prevention and treatment of blisters)
- triangular bandage (for holding dressings in place, attaching splints, and creating slings)
- hand cleaner

Equipment and Accessories
- tweezers
- needle
- single-sided razor blade
- bandage scissors
- irrigation syringe
- low-reading thermometer
- SAM Splint or wire mesh
- cold pack
- space blanket
- waterproof matches
- emergency phone numbers and money for a phone call
- bee-sting kit
- snakebite kit: compress, suction (use a Sawyer Kit)
- dental kit: oil of cloves, cotton pads, wax
- 2 pair of latex gloves
- plastic bags
- small flashlight and extra batteries

**Medicines and Drugs: Pain Relief Drugs
and Topical Applications.**
Check with all students for any allergic history to any of these
drugs.
● Aspirin: mild analgesic; anti-inflammatory, reduces fever;
interferes with blood clotting; can cause nausea; don't give to
children.
● Motrin®: anti-inflammatory and moderate pain relief; may
cause stomach irritation and nausea.
● Tylenol®: for relief of minor to moderate pain such as muscle
ache and inflammation; may cause liver damage in excessive
doses; first choice for pain relief in many first-aid kits.

Allergic Reaction Drugs and Topical Applications
● Benadryl®: acts as an antihistamine, sedative, and anti-itch
treatment. Use with caution; may cause drowsiness, constipa-
tion, weakness, headache, difficulty in urination, diarrhea.
● Ana-Kit: injection of epinephrine and Chlo-Amine® tablets
to relieve severe allergic reaction. May cause headache, anxiety,
heart palpitations.
● Caladryl® lotion: a calamine and Benadryl lotion to relieve
minor skin irritations.
● Hydrocortisone ointment (2.5 percent): Steroid ointment for
more severe skin reactions.

Gastrointestinal Medications
● Lomotil®: controls diarrhea. Use only if the diarrhea com-
promises safety or an ability to travel, for it is possible to
introduce serious infection and start a fever because of bowel
retention.
● Maalox®: Neutralizes stomach acids and relieves indigestion.
Can produce mild diarrhea.

Antibiotic and Antiseptic Ointments
● Neosporin Ointment: Helps prevent infection in minor cuts
and abrasions.
● Betadine®: Use for topical cleaning of skin around the

wound or before lancing a blister. If using to clean a wound, use 25 percent Betadine to 75 percent sterile water. Never use Betadine in a deep wound.

Skin Preparation
● Tincture of Benzoin: Prepares skin for application of adhesive.

Other Drugs to Consider
● Cough suppressant: For example, Robitussin® with codeine.
● Decongestant: For example, Afrin® Nasal Spray (not recommended for prolonged periods or for use at high altitudes).
● Antibiotic Eye Drops: For example, Neosporin Ophthalmic Drops.
● Skin Care: For example, A & D Ointment®, which soothes rashes and dry skin. Be sure to check the first-aid kit regularly to discard any out-of-date items. Design your first aid to fit your specific activities.

Informing Parents and Supervisors

COMMON CAUSES OF CHOKING

Trying to swallow large pieces of poorly chewed food.

Eating while talking excitedly or laughing or eating too fast.

Walking, playing, or running with food or objects in mouth.

Parents must know about any injury their son or daughter sustains while under the supervision of the youth ministry. Even small injuries should motivate the youth leader to meet the parents at the car when they come to pick up their son or daughter. A quick explanation of what happened and how the injury was treated gives parents information and builds confidence that their young people are being properly supervised.

When the accident is more serious and requires an ambulance or a trip to the emergency room, the parents must be called. It is better for the parents to hear from the youth worker prior to a hospital worker calling to confirm insurance coverage or requesting permission to treat the injury.

There is no subtle or clever way to deliver the news of injury to a parent. Direct and clear is the best style. Don't drag out the information. They want to hear the bottom line: how their son or daughter is right now. Here is a sample conversation:

"Hello, Mrs. Jones, this is Jack Crabtree from the youth ministry down at the church. Please don't be alarmed. I am just calling to tell you that Danny took a fall tonight in the church gym and hurt his arm. He is in good shape, but he is having a lot of pain in that arm. So we decided to bring him to the hospital emergency room for X-rays and treatment. We are here at the hospital right now getting him checked in. I just wanted to let you know what is happening."

That's not too hard! The injury at worst is a broken bone. You would stay on the phone to answer any question the parents would have and give information about how they can find you and come to see their son.

Let's try a harder one: "Hello, Mrs. Collins, this is Jack Crabtree, from the youth ministry bike trip. I am calling to let you know Brian was injured about an hour ago. He took a pretty nasty fall on his bike just outside of Albany. We're at the hospital right now. I don't know the full extent of his injuries, but the ambulance guys told me he is conscious and doing pretty well. He is getting excellent care. The hospital has all the medical information you gave us about Brian, so the doctors will be calling you shortly. I will get off the phone so you can receive that call. Here's the number of the phone I am using to call you. You can call me or I'll stay on as long as you would like to talk. I'll call you with every piece of news I get from the doctors."

It is very important for the family to know how to contact you. Remember to give them the number of a phone at which you can be reached. Stay calm. Don't raise any speculation about the young person's condition—positive or negative—without solid evidence to support it. Reassure the parents of the care their son or daughter is receiving and of your commitment to keep them informed.

The next call you need to make is to your superior or supervisor in the youth ministry. Give him or her the essential facts about what happened and how you are handling the situation. If you are at a bank of pay phones, use another phone so the parents can call back and get through to you (a mother or father will often call back immediately after calling their spouse). Your youth ministry superior can help you think through what you are doing and any logistic problems you might have. You can pray together for God's hand to be on everyone involved. Keep the line of communication open with your superior. Even in the simpler situation of a sprain or broken bone, if you take someone to the emergency room it is wise to call your supervisor. He or she can help you think through everything you should do. Discuss with your supervisor beforehand how any accident should be handled.

After any accident and treatment the youth ministry worker should write (that's right—pencil and paper!) a report describing what happened to cause the injury, what was done at the scene of the accident, and any additional treatment given by a hospital or doctor. Ask any witnesses to the accident to write or give you a verbal statement (write word-for-word what they say) about what they saw happen. (See the form in the appendix.)

MISSED THE TURN

Pete held in his anger. He had just missed the turn, but he wasn't going to lose it in front of his youth group riding with him in the church van. Now he had to turn around and wait through a couple long traffic lights.

During the second light there was some serious stirring in the back seat of the van. He stared into the rearview mirror to see his wife Joan leave her seat to join the girls in the way back.

He heard Joan's voice, "Pete, get us to a hospital quick." Pete turned into the convenience store next to the traffic light and quickly asked directions. In three minutes they were at the hospital. Joan pulled a young girl from that back seat holding her throat and gasping for air and rushed through the emergency room doors.

The young girl was having a severe allergic reaction to some pollen she had contacted during their day hike. She felt her throat swelling and gradually closing, making it difficult to breathe. She might not have survived another 20 minutes.

Pete thanked God for two specific blessings. His wife Joan was a registered nurse and his best female counselor. He never took a youth group trip without her. Tonight she was a lifesaver. The second blessing—that missed turn. Without it they would have been down the ramp and onto the interstate highway miles from the hospital and a place to turn around when the breathing emergency happened. What would have happened then?

If the young person stays under your supervision for the days following, keep notes about his or her condition and recovery. Check on the student regularly. Stay in touch with the parents, giving regular reports to them. Call them with the student and ask the parents what they want you to do and how often they want you to call. It is better to call too often than too little. Keep a written record of all the calls. Combine these notes with your notes on the person's condition and submit them to your superior when you return home.

Checking back regularly with the student and the family builds good relations and provides evidence that you care about what caused the student's injury. Feeling forgotten or ignored angers parents and stimulates lawsuits.

Within a couple weeks, review the entire situation with your supervisor to debrief what happened, how you responded, and what lasting impact will be felt in the ministry. Make this a learning experience to sharpen your safety procedures and first-aid response. You might want to institute some new training for your workers or change how a certain event is conducted. The whole process will make you and your youth ministry a safer environment.

CHAPTER ELEVEN
When the Worst Happens

The worst day of my life was Monday, August 20, 1990. We were halfway through our YFC/Campus Life bicycle tour with 50 students and staff riding round trip from Long Island (N.Y.) to Maine. This day's outing was a light ride to Ogunquit, Maine (20 miles each way) for a fun day at the ocean.

We never made it to the beach. As the adult leader I was riding in the next-to-last spot in the single file line of eight bikers. My experienced college-age leader was in front, leading the way. I was doing my job, reminding the riders about being careful and warning them about the traffic approaching from behind.

Suddenly Kim Masterson, one of the young women riding in the middle of our single file line, lost her balance and began to fall to her left into the road. The more she fought to regain her balance the deeper her bike veered into the traffic. Everything seemed to go into slow motion as we watched a vehicle collide with Kim. That sequence is still a clear picture in my mind even though over three years have passed.

I jumped from my bike and rushed to Kim, who was lying on the road. Checking her vital signs, I could not detect any indication of life. A doctor at the hospital would later confirm that she had died instantly from massive multiple traumas. In the midst of indescribable chaos, I quickly checked to see if anyone else in the group had been injured and organized them to call an ambulance, stop the traffic, and begin helping me.

I quickly prayed for Kim and asked God to give me the strength and wisdom I needed for that moment. I began rescue breathing and CPR while trying to control the bleeding and other apparent injuries in an attempt to give Kim every chance I could to restore her vital signs. The ambulance crew arrived within 15 minutes and took over the treatment.

While I attended to Kim, the junior leader had found a motorist with a car phone to call the emergency number. The traffic had stopped in both directions. I remember seeing women leave their cars to come to the aid of the students in our group. The students who had not been assigned a job were shaking and crying. These ladies embraced these young people and comforted them as the emergency procedures continued. One of our guys ran back up the road to stop the next approaching bike group. I had told him to keep them at least 200 feet away from the scene.

When Kim was placed in the ambulance, a police detective asked me to ride with him to the hospital. I quickly ran back to the bike group leaders who had been sitting in hushed silence 200 feet away and gave them instructions to work out all the necessary logistics. The police were outstanding in the way they helped us solve all the problems this accident presented. On the way to the hospital I spotted our support van sitting in the stalled traffic. When I stepped out of the police car, their worst fears were confirmed. From the files in the van I pulled all the information we had on Kim to take with me to the hospital. The staff in the van were given clearance to move ahead and work with the police to help the remaining bikers.

My head was spinning. My heart was breaking. I stiffened every part of my insides to try and maintain control of myself. At the hospital the confirmation of Kim's death came quickly. In 19 years of youth work I had always prayed to never be in a hospital room and hear those words. The impact of what Kim's death would mean to her family and everyone involved began to hit me hard.

I was driven to the police station where we started the paper work and the process of contacting Kim's parents back on Long Island. I called their pastor with the news. He traveled with the Long Island police (who had been contacted by the Maine police) to the parents' place of business. They delivered the bad news to Kim's mom and dad and then called me at the Maine police station. I had always chided kids on previous trips when I warned them about safety, telling them I would not know what to say if I ever had to call their parents. It was even more difficult than I had expected. The police sergeant stood beside me and coached me through the call. Kim's parents were so thoughtful in their shock and grief to express their concern for me and everyone on the trip.

My next calls were to the Long Island YFC office, our local board chairman, and my wife. They started the process of informing the national YFC office and all the parents of students on the trip. While I was calling Long Island, the police sergeant was contacting a local youth agency to request help for our group.

This was a key moment in the whole process. I would have never thought of requesting such help, especially from a secular agency. I needed plenty of help, but the emotional tidal wave sweeping over me hindered my ability to function rationally to determine what needed to be done. I was already experiencing a "walking shock" and was in no position to do any more than I had already been trained to do. The police sergeant had taken me through his part of the process and now had the compassion and foresight to pass me on to the people who could help me face the problems still ahead.

Response to Sudden Death
At this point the focus of this story shifts from the accident to the response of a team of counselors from a variety of agencies who came together to provide emergency care for us. Their response provides a model for helping youth groups who have experienced a sudden death or a severe injury while on a trip away from home.

Within an hour of making the phone calls I was in a local hospital meeting with a team of six mental health care workers and counselors. They were prepared to help me develop a plan to take the news of Kim's death back to our group. All the students and staff had been returned by bus to the youth home where we had stayed the previous night. They helped me plan the logistics of canceling the trip and returning home. The team spent the first hour of the meeting drawing information from me to understand the special counseling needs our students would require during the 24 hours before we traveled home. The coordinator of the team showed great sensitivity toward our Christian faith. One of the people they selected for the team was from a local Christian counseling center. The fact that he had served as a YFC director some years prior helped the other workers understand our group. All of them showed generous love and care for me and the burdens I carried during those hours.

The police called ahead before returning me to the youth home where all the students and staff were waiting for some word from me about Kim. They arranged a quick entrance into the building for me and an immediate meeting with half of the staff and some of Kim's closest friends. After meeting with them, we met with the rest of the staff and finally gathered the whole group to break the news. The team of counselors accompanied me and coached me as I delivered the bad news in each session. They spread themselves among the staff and young people and helped them to talk about their feelings.

For 19 hours (from 4 P.M. until 11 A.M. the next morning when we boarded the chartered bus) the team of counselors from local agencies were on site with us, available to talk and comfort anyone who needed help. The team broke our group into significant subgroups accordingly to the impact of the accident on each person. They assigned counselors to each group and responded accordingly to the needs they observed.

Our biking group (seven of us) met in a private room with the team coordinator to discuss what had happened to us. This group was the most deeply traumatized because we had seen the accident and been present through the emergency efforts. The counselor asked us to agree to talk about what we had seen only within our group. There was no need for others on the trip to know the details of the tragedy we had witnessed firsthand. We were then asked to share in full detail what we saw happen that morning. It was hard for everyone to speak aloud. Earlier a woman at the police department had given me six large teddy bears to give to any of Kim's special friends. At the time I thought the gift was totally inappropriate, but at the counselor's suggestion I distributed them in our group. Having something soft to hold and squeeze seemed to help some people get out the words and the tears.

When I shared with the group, my whole body shook uncontrollably as I described what I saw and did at the scene of the accident. Later that night when I struggled to stay awake (I was afraid of having a nightmare), I wandered into the dining room and spoke with a counselor. Half of our group stayed up most of the night talking, playing board games, and spending time with the counselors. As much as I hated it, talking about the details did bring some relief.

The next morning we had a large group meeting with some singing and testimonies about Kim and her strong Christian faith. We concluded with a short talk about what the Bible says about death and what happened to Kim when she died.

The counseling team stayed with us until we were loaded on the bus. They gave instruction to us about what we would experience in the days ahead. They helped us realize that our intense feelings were quite normal. It felt like leaving special friends when we said goodbye.

It was a seven-hour bus ride home. While our emotions had been drained during the 24 hours in Maine, we were greeted by parents and friends who were bursting with emotion. Every family situation was highly charged with a variety of feelings. No one could escape what had happened to us. The wake (viewing) and the funeral the next three days were a roller coaster of feelings and experiences. We were drawing on our Christian faith for all it could provide. At the same time we were having feelings and thoughts that were entirely different than any we had ever known in the past. Kim's parents greeted us lovingly and showed great concern for our needs. Their support and kindness buoyed our YFC staff.

The night after the funeral, we held an open house at a local church for any student or parent who wanted to attend. Counselors from a local hospital who specialized in assisting victims of trauma volunteered their services. The next few Friday nights we gathered many students from the trip together for times of games, music, snacks, and talk.

After Kim's funeral the group most resistant to counseling was the staff. We had several all-staff sessions where the counselors found it very difficult to get the staff members to share their feelings. We stopped after two sessions at the request of the staff. I personally went to a counselor weekly for four months and felt the benefit of opening up with him.

For all my experience in planning bike trips, I had never considered a contingency plan for a death or serious injury. I would never have considered how a team of local counselors could help our group. They helped us release our thoughts and emotions with their quiet, listening style. Our staff was supported by these professionals and taught how to respond to a sudden death. In less than 24 hours they gave us a foundation from which we could step off into the grieving process. The team of trauma counselors who met with us when

THE REST OF THE STORY . . .

In the months following the biking accident we saw a wide variety of reactions and behaviors in students and staff. I couldn't always explain it, but I knew the accident had something to do with how a person was feeling and acting. Even though I had ridden over 15,000 miles on organized trips, my fear was so strong it took me six months to get back on a bicycle. Each day was loaded with flashbacks.

The next summer we ran a shorter, seven-day bike trip. It was one of the safest trips we have ever conducted. We used the same safety rules, but the students believed our warnings and practiced self enforcement.

The Masterson family continues to be absolutely super to me and the staff. They have been loving, forgiving, and kind to all of us who were involved.

we returned home helped us handle our feelings about the funeral and the tensions we felt when we reentered our families. Each group played a special role at a crucial time. Some staff and students took advantage of their services, others did not. It was important to have these services available.

How the Counseling Teams Helped Our Group

They helped the leader by:
- providing practical help and emotional support
- coordinating logistics (arranged food, buses, phone calls)
- formulating a 24-hour plan
- providing personal counseling ·

They prepared a counseling strategy by:
- dividing people into groups according to the level of trauma
- taking leadership with each of the groups
- devising a strategy to break the news sensitively to the group ·
- responding to special people and their needs

They educated the staff by:
- helping them deal with their own grief
- teaching them how to help others handle their grief
- telling them what to expect in the days and weeks ahead

Preparing for Traumatic Situations

Obviously no one knows when a tragedy will strike his or her group. The responsibility of the leader is to provide emergency preparedness for the youth ministry staff and the youth of the church. It's normal not to seek help until you need it, but it is wise to be prepared for the worst. Emergency preparedness does not only apply to accidental deaths, but also to suicides and disabling injuries that might occur in the group.

Who Can Help Us Respond?

Which hospital in your area has a trauma team? Familiarize yourself with their services. Keep their phone number and contact names in your personal records and in the church records.

The key person to find is a competent trauma team coordinator. This person should know how to respond and should be aware of the resources in the community. The youth group leader cannot put all the pieces of logistics, counseling, and response together when he or she is part of the tragedy. Plan ahead by identifying several people in your community who could fill that role.

Other sources of help include:

HOW TO SURVIVE A TRAUMATIC EXPERIENCE

1 Don't be afraid to cry.

2. Find someone who is a good listener.

3. Take time to heal.

4. Expect setbacks.

5. Don't make any major decisions.

6. Get involved in a support group.

Iris Bolton
Know You Can Survive

• hot lines: keep a list of contacts and specific specialty services they offer.

• police, fire, and emergency squads: they offer not only immediate assistance, but they also know additional community resources who can help.

• organizations such as Compassionate Friends and Survivor Groups: check their listings in the phone book.

• prayer chains—what churches in your area have active prayer organizations that can quickly mobilize people to pray for a traumatic situation? Keep their phone numbers readily available.

• therapists and counselors: who in your community is trained and willing to help in an emergency?

• ministers: who in your community is trained or experienced in counseling people through grief and trauma? Compile a list.

• health care professionals on church or organization boards: these people are close to ministry and have professional skills to offer.

• bereavement groups: where can students and staff find long-term support?

Prepare to Educate Students and Staff

Given the probability of some traumatic event happening to

your youth group or a student in your group, it is good planning to prepare an information sheet on what they can expect to experience. This sheet can be given to them at the appropriate time with the verbal counseling you or a professional counselor will provide. Here's a sample:

Traumatic Event Stress Information Sheet

You have experienced a traumatic event. Even though the event may be over, you may still be experiencing strong emotional or physical reactions. It is very common and quite normal for people to experience a stress reaction or emotional aftershocks. These aftershocks can appear immediately or be delayed over a wide period of time.

The signs and symptoms of a stress reaction or emotional aftershock may last any length of time depending on the severity of the trauma you experienced. Sometimes just having the understanding and support of caring friends can help you through the stress reaction. Other times the traumatic event can be so strong that you may need to talk with a professional counselor. It doesn't mean you are crazy or weak. What you experienced is just more than one person can handle.

Here are common signs and signals of a stress reaction:

Feelings
- *anxiety*
- *guilt*
- *grief*
- *denial*
- *emotional shock*
- *fear*
- *uncertainty*
- *loss of emotional control*
- *depression*
- *feeling overwhelmed*
- *intense anger*
- *irritable*

Thoughts
- *blaming someone/yourself*
- *confusion*
- *poor attention*
- *poor decisions*
- *poor concentration*
- *change in alertness*
- *memory problems*
- *poor problem solving*
- *disorientation*
- *disturbed thinking*
- *nightmares*

Physical
- *fatigue*
- *nausea*
- *muscles tremors*
- *twitches*
- *chest pain**
- *difficult breathing**
- *elevated blood pressure*
- *profuse sweating*
- *fainting*
- *rapid heart beat*
- *thirst*
- *headaches*
- *vomiting*
- *grinding of teeth*
- *weakness*
- *dizziness*
- *chills*

*seek immediate medical treatment

Behavior
- *withdrawal*
- *emotional outbursts*
- *change in usual habits of communication*
- *increased alcohol consumption*
- *suspiciousness*
- *inability to rest*
- *hyperalert to environment*
- *easily startled*
- *change in appetite*
- *pacing*
- *erratic movements*
- *panic or anxiety attacks*

How to Deal with Emotional Aftershocks
- Within the first 24–48 hours, perform some strenuous physical exercise alternated with relaxation.
- Structure your time and keep busy.
- Realize you are normal and your reactions are normal.
- Talk to people. Talking is the most healing medicine.
- Don't try to numb your pain with drugs or alcohol.
- Reach out to people who are trying to help you.
- Maintain a normal schedule.
- Spend time with others.
- Keep a journal and write your way through the sleepless hours.
- Don't make any big decisions.
- Get plenty of rest.
- Accept recurring thoughts, dreams, and flashbacks as normal. Don't fight them. They will decrease over time and

become less painful.

- Eat well-balanced and regular meals (even when you don't feel like it).
- Share your feelings and thoughts with others.

Helping a Friend or Family Member Go through Emotional Aftershock

- Listen carefully.
- Spend time with the person.
- Offer assistance and a listening ear.
- Reassure the person that he or she is safe.
- Help with everyday tasks.
- Give the person some private time.
- Don't take the affected person's anger or other feelings personally.
- Don't tell the person that he or she was "lucky it wasn't worse." Traumatized people are not consoled by such statements.
- Tell the person you are sorry the event happened and that you want to understand and assist him or her.
- Remind the person that confusing emotions are normal.
- Don't attempt to impose your explanation on why the event happened.
- Don't tell the person you know how it feels. You probably don't.
- Be willing to say nothing. Just being there is often the best help you can give.
- Go to any meetings or appointments that concern the event. Offer to go and support him or her.
- Don't ask for details of the trauma. If the person wants to talk, just listen. Let him or her know you are there and you care. It isn't necessary to try and make things better. Offer to pray with them and for them.
- Read passages of assurance and hope from the Bible.

Dealing with a Suicide in or Near Your Group

The friends and family of a person who commits suicide go

through a similar bereavement process. They are overwhelmed by the intensity of their feelings. They often feel very angry at the person for ending his or her life. There is guilt and remorse over what should have been done to help the person. They recognize calls for help that they overlooked prior to the suicide. The survivors often feel hopeless and depressed.

Dealing with the survivors starts with encouraging them to express their feelings. Provide places to talk and comfortable ways to bring up the subject. Teach the survivors about the grief process so they can understand that their feelings are normal. Help them call upon their faith in God. Stress God's plan and purpose for them. Encourage them to participate in a weekly support group for several months or more. If necessary, arrange for them to seek professional help.

Dealing with a Disabling Injury

Some people believe that a disabling injury is even more stressful than a death because of the long term impact it has on the lives of everyone involved. The shock of such an injury is similar to what people feel when someone is killed. The last step of the grieving process is reconciling to the new situation and deciding to move ahead. A disabled person and the family have to go through the same process to reach that conclusion.

There are increasing numbers of books and helpful training classes to assist people in reacting to such injuries and adjusting to living productive lives. Support groups of people who have had similar experiences are available to friends and family members to provide a place to vent their feelings and frustrations.

Returning to "Normal"

After a death or a disabling injury, it is almost impossible to return to ministry the way it was before the event. Spiritually, the best place to start is where the group finds itself. The lessons can be refocused to give attention to the issues raised by the accident. The format of the ministry should include more opportunities for open and honest sharing. When the awkward moments come, just acknowledge how everyone is feeling and move ahead with a positive statement about the person and what the group has been through. The goal is to help everyone reconcile to the fact of the accident and move forward. The example of the leader can set the tone for the group. If the leader acknowledges his or her need for help, seeks counseling, and talks openly about what happened, it helps the attitude of the whole group.

Can you return to the same activity or location of the accident? We were encouraged by Kim's parents to continue our bike trips. Their vocal support made it a much easier decision. We reexamined our safety procedures and committed ourselves to continue our high standards of safety. Since the accident, we have conducted two long trips without incident. Approximately half of the students who were on the trip when the accident occurred have ridden with us again. We have tried to create an atmosphere where we can talk about our fears and feelings openly. We're moving ahead. It's been a real-life lesson in overcoming fear.

I hope you won't ever have a young person killed during one of your youth ministry activities. Hopefully my story has motivated you to commit your best efforts to protecting the health and safety of your students. If, despite your best efforts, a student is killed or disabled, I hope this account provides an outline for dealing with the tragedy. You can be confident that God will provide the strength you need in those trying moments.

CHAPTER TWELVE
"Dear Lord, Guard and Protect Us"

How safety conscious was Jesus? Imagine His reaction if one of His disciples had the courage to speak up when Jesus was inviting Peter to step off the edge of the boat and on to the water. "Excuse me, Jesus, shouldn't Peter be wearing a personal flotation device approved by the Roman Legion Coast Guard?"

Does being strong on safety practices contradict the life of faith we are trying to live? Should safety procedures and practices be a big concern to us if we are strong in prayer, believe the Bible, and are led by the Spirit?

For many youth workers the subjects of safety and spirituality pose no contradictions. It's not either/or; it's both/and. But for those in youth work who do hold on to faith and prayer as their only line of safety and to those others who hide their lazy safety habits behind a theological screen, here are six often asked questions.

Does Living by Faith Mean Taking Safety Risks?

Praying prayers of faith and practicing common sense don't contradict each other. A mature Christian seeks to develop a growing, integrated package of common sense, spirituality, and wisdom. Even though we build our youth ministry on God's Word and prayer, we don't need a Bible passage or a prayer session to convince us that we need to wear a life jacket in

197

deep, fast water. God is good. He gave us a brain to handle some of the obvious choices of daily life.

A secular man and a spiritual man standing on the bank of the river deciding if their respective youth groups should go in the water should reach the same conclusion. The spiritual man hasn't demonstrated any lack of faith by deciding not to canoe the river. In fact, the spiritual man has even better reasons for his decision than the secular man who operates strictly on a common sense basis.

The spiritual man has the benefit of knowing that the lives under his responsibility are special, unique creations of God. He recognizes the fallen world as a dangerous place with pain, suffering, and death caused by rebellion against God. He lives his life to glorify God and to reflect the character of God to everyone he contacts. He realizes handling young lives carelessly does not reflect the character of God.

Can't God Protect Us? Why Should We Try to Protect Ourselves?

Some people argue that the Christian life is built on putting our trust in God alone, not by following the conventions of human beings. Therefore, they say, the Christian youth program operating by faith can take risks because God will guide and protect.

Don't believe it! God is capable of rescuing people from any hazardous situation, but that does not mean we should tempt Him or defy the forces of nature. In the desert, Satan challenged Jesus to throw himself off the top on the temple because God would provide angels to catch him. Jesus replied, "It is written 'Do not put the Lord your God to the test.'" Conducting youth ministry without a safety plan and depending on God solely to protect us is putting God to the test. That's not faith—it's foolishness.

Will God protect us when we don't plan for safety or use common sense? That's the wrong question. The real question is "Are we wise or are we foolish?"

"He who trusts in himself is a fool, but he who walks in wisdom is kept safe" (Prov. 28:26).

What does it mean to walk in wisdom?

1. To trust and honor God.
2. To know what God has said in His Word.
3. To make right choices.
4. To learn from our mistakes.

The spiritual, safety-conscious youth leader walks in wisdom. Prayer is central along with learning what God wants us to know from the lessons of life. From our experiences we develop common sense. When you reflect God's character and values, safety becomes a strong motivation. We plan for safety because every young life is valued and treasured by God. If God cares for them, shouldn't we use every ounce of our ability to do the same. How could any young person believe they are loved by God when at the same time youth ministry leaders who represent God to them are putting them in dangerous situations with little regard for their safety?

The wise youth worker prays diligently about the safety of his or her students, calling on God to point out what needs to be done to protect each young person. This leader learns from his or her own mistakes and by listening to others. He or she sets aside pride and ego to gain a teachable attitude. Reading this book provides youth workers with true-life stories from which lessons can be learned. Being wise means learning lessons and applying them to the way we live.

Can't We Just Pray and Go for It?

I was speaking at a youth workers training session during the initial stages of preparing the material for this book. I shared with the group the story of Larry (see chapter 1), the youth director who had to decide if he would take his youth group canoeing in a swollen river. I paused just before revealing Larry's decision and asked the 85 youth leaders what they would do.

One lively, strapping guy said, "I'd get those kids out of the van. We'd have some serious prayer time and then go for it."

The other leaders exploded with response. Half seemed energized by his spiritual enthusiasm and confidence that God hears prayers and watches over his children when they step out in faith. The other half seemed shocked at the suggestion of exposing young people to such an obvious risk.

The questions bounced off the walls. What kind of serious prayer session does it take to get inexperienced canoeists safely down a swollen river? How do you know if your prayer time has been serious enough? Does serious prayer mean talking loud and long to God or listening quietly and carefully to God? One leader in the training session wanted to know if this was really a serious prayer session, wouldn't God tell someone in that circle that it wasn't safe for them to be in the river?

We misunderstand prayer when we treat it like a magic insurance policy. We can't do whatever we want and expect God to protect us just because we got two or three to agree in Jesus' name. This is a fundamental issue of prayer. Do we pray to tell God what we want Him to do for us or are we supposed to be listening for some indication of what He wants us to do for Him?

The right kind of prayer for a leader to pray sounds something like this: "Lord, as we lead this youth ministry, point out to us what is ungodly, unproductive, and unsafe. Show us how to change it so we will take care of these young people the way You would and be a better witness for Your name."

How Can Safety Be a Witness for Jesus?

In the scores of interviews conducted with youth ministry leaders for this book, there was always a "part two" with every "accident" story they told. What was their future relationship with the student and the family after the incident? Many told us of students and parents turned off to the church and the Christian faith when they felt the youth ministry had put them (or their child) in jeopardy.

The students who were betrayed sexually or abused physically had the most severe reaction to their leaders. Many of them sunk into deep rebellion against God and doubted the sincerity of any Christian leader. Those who were hurt physically during ministry activities were more forgiving. But in situations where the parents felt the youth leaders were careless or too nonchalant about safety, the walls went up between the youth ministry and the whole family.

All of us in youth ministry staff need to hear Jesus' warning with fresh ears: "But if anyone causes one of these little ones who believe in me to sin, it would be better for him to have a large millstone hung around his neck and to be drowned in the depths of the sea" (Matt. 18:6). God will drop the hammer on those who seduce and abuse kids sexually and physically. It is also justified to extend this warning to youth leaders who harden the hearts of young people and parents toward God because of youth ministry incidents that lacked care and responsibility.

Safety is a positive witness to young people and especially to their parents. If you are attempting to be a witness for Christ to a unchurched family, one of the very best ways to create interest and involvement is to demonstrate how much you care for their children. In 20 years of leading bike trips, I have seen parents positively impacted for Christ because they saw dedicated concern and care for their teenager by our adult leaders. The skill and professionalism we demonstrated through the discipline of the trip and the care provided when their young person was ill or injured won the admiration and interest of the parents.

All the young people in our groups are precious resources entrusted to us by God (and their parents) for care and handling. How we treat them shapes their lives. We cannot accept any policy of safety that treats kids less safely than their parents would treat them. Living up to God's treatment standards is even more challenging.

Maybe Accidents and Injuries Are God's Will

Another leader at the training session raised the question, "Whatever happened to the sovereignty of God? We can't be worrying about everything that might happen to our kids. What's wrong with just trusting that whatever happens is the will of God?" Are we trying to do God's job by being so paranoid about safety?

When Kim Masterson was killed on our bicycle trip I asked a thousand "what if" and "why" questions. The original plan for the trip had us riding on that stretch of road the day before the actual accident. It poured heavy rain that day. We had an extra day on our schedule and made the decision not to put ourselves on the road in those conditions. The day of the accident was bright and sunny. If we had ridden the previous day in the rain and had taken the sunny day off, would we have avoided the accident and Kim's death? Kim was a last minute registrant on the trip, headed for her freshman year of college as soon as she returned home. If she had been home preparing for college on that day would she have died in different circumstances? Had God appointed that day as her last day on earth? Was it God's will for Kim to die on that day on a road in Maine? I don't think I'll ever know the answers to those questions while I am alive on this earth.

I do have great confidence in the sovereignty of God. I believe that God works out all things for our good. It doesn't mean that everything that happens to us is good. The evil in our fallen world produces an environment that includes pain, suffering, and death. What is remarkable is God's ability to use even these terrible events for our long-term good. In our hedonist world I need a constant reminder that God is not working to make me happy, but to fulfill His purpose.

Yet my confidence in the sovereignty of God is no reason to relax my best human efforts to keep everyone on a bicycle trip safe from danger. Life is precious, and my job (both inside and outside of youth ministry) is to protect it.

I challenge those who would argue the sovereignty of God as a reason for not giving our best effort for safety. Do you leave your house unlocked and believe that if it is God's will for your house to be robbed, it will happen regardless of what precautions you might take? Most people don't! They trust God to provide protection, but they do their part by installing and using locks on the doors to keep their cars and houses from being burglarized.

It is godly common sense to recognize the dangers of this world and respond appropriately. If we love our money and our valuables and take steps to protect them, can we say we love young people when we don't take even more precautions to protect the ones God has placed in our care? We recognize the dangers and observe safety procedures because we don't want to lose any of them. Our safety efforts in youth ministry should not be any different than what we practice with our most precious material possessions.

We live in a fallen world. It is governed by physical laws and natural forces. We plan our steps according to those forces. Although God is both capable and caring, you can't plan your youth ministry with the expectation that God will suspend the laws of physics or the force of gravity when you shoot up a 911 prayer.

God gave us the task (and responsibility) of dominating the earth. Part of that task requires us to familiarize ourselves with how the world works and to teach ourselves and others how to respond. We learn about our environment and stay away from dangerous activities. Even strong Christians don't hold a prayer service in the middle of a lake holding up a large metal cross during a thunderstorm.

When Accidents Happen, Has God Failed Us?

A friend told me I shouldn't be praying for safety in front of the students in our youth group. She is concerned that students might lose faith in God's ability to answer our prayers if we have an accident and someone is hurt or killed.

If an accident happens, does it mean God didn't hear our prayers for safety? Perhaps we should thank God that nothing worse happened to our group. Maybe we were shielded from seeing how God protected us from a greater disaster. Perhaps we are guilty of taking for granted all the instances of God's protection each day that we don't see. We need to keep praying with intensity for God's hand to be on all we do.

After an accident some students and staff may feel strongly that God doesn't care. When Job struggled through his calamities he learned that it's not always possible to understand the reasons why they occurred. Sometimes the answers and explanations are held back. Believing in God or prayer does not protect us from trouble. Rather, it prepares us to handle what life in a fallen world brings to us. The message of Job is not to give up. God may allow suffering in our lives for reasons we can't understand. Through the whole process our faith and trust in God can grow.

Jay Kesler, president of Taylor University, has said when we see some tragic accident happen we have three choices: 1) we can believe there is no God; 2) we can believe God causes these things to happen; or 3) we can understand that God allows these things to happen without causing them. God has created a physical universe with natural laws that govern how we live. Sometimes gravity saves a person's life; other times gravity pulls a person to his or her death. Everything we know about God tells us that when accidents happen, God is as sad about the injuries or deaths as the people who are involved.

Final Thoughts

For people to believe the message of God's love, they must trust the messenger. God has placed youth ministers in a strategic position to change the lives of entire families. Their mission begins with trust. If parents and students know the youth ministry staff care so much for them that their top priority is to protect their safety, they will be open to the message they bring. Lack of planning and care for safety is not only criminal, it is a terrible witness for Christ.

Attention to safety concerns brings glory to the name of Christ. It shows love and concern. It lays the foundation for future trust when the life changing message of Jesus is presented. Safety concerns are not a contradiction to a life of faith. In youth ministry, safety concerns open the door for people to discover a life of faith.

Appendix

Sample Health Form

(Name of Church or Youth Ministry)
Mandatory Health Form

(Please Print)

Name of Student _____ Date of Birth _____

Address _____ Age _____

Town _____ State _____ Zip _____

Phone # (___) _____ Sex _____ Height _____ Weight _____

Social Security # _____

Emergency Contact Person:

Parent/Guardian Name _____

Address (if different from student) _____

Town _____ State _____ Zip _____

Phone # (Home) (_____) _____ (Work) (_____) _____

Alternate Contact Person: *(Use someone near the primary contact)*

Name _____

Address _____

Town _____ State _____ Zip _____

Phone # (Home) (_____) _____ (Work) (_____) _____

Sample Health Form—Page 2

If you have medical insurance, your carrier will be billed for medical charges in the case of illness or injury while your child is at the activity.

Do you have health insurance? ___ Yes ___ No

Name of insurance company _____

Policy # _____ ___ Group # _____

In whose name is the insurance? _____

Family Doctor _____ City/Town _____ Phone # _____

If your child should require medical attention for injuries received or illnesses contracted prior to activity, please send us the necessary information to give him/her proper medical care during his/her time with the youth ministry activity.

Health History:

Any pre-existing or present medical conditions:

_____

_____

Name and dosage of any medications that must be taken _____

_____

Any allergies? _____ to Medications? _____

___ Hay Fever   ___ Heart Condition   ___ Diabetes

___ Insect Stings   ___ Epilepsy/Nervous Disorders   ___ Asthma

___ Frequent Stomach Upsets   ___ Physical Handicap

Sample Health Form—Page 3

___ Any Major Illnesses During the Past Year?

If any of the above are checked, please give details (i.e., include normal treatment of allergic reactions)

_____

_____

Date of last Tetanus shot _____ Contact Lenses? _____

Any swimming restrictions? ___ Yes ___ No What? _____

Any activity restrictions? ___ Yes ___ No What? _____

Parent Medical and Liability Release Statement:

I understand that in the event medical intervention is needed, every attempt will be made to contact immediately the persons listed on this form. In the event I cannot be reached in an emergency during the activity dates shown on this form, I hereby give my permission to the physician or dentist selected by the activity leader to hospitalize, to secure medical treatment and/or order an injection, anesthesia, or surgery for my child as deemed necessary.

I understand all reasonable safety precautions will be taken at all times by the (name of the church or organization) and its agents during the events and activities. I understand the possibility of unforeseen hazards and know the inherent possibility of risk. I agree not to hold (name of church or organization), its leaders, employees, and volunteer staff liable for damages, losses, diseases, or injuries incurred by the subject of this form.

Parent/Guardian Signature _____ Date _____

Signature of Student (if over 18 years of age) _____

Notarized

Parent Information and Release Form

(Name of Church or Youth Ministry)
Parent/Guardian Information and Permission Form
Name of Activity and Dates

(Please Print)

Name of Student _____ Date of Birth _____

Address _____ Age _____

Town _____ State _____ Zip _____

Phone # (____) _____ Sex _____

Student Information and Code of Behavior Agreement
Description of the activity/event and dates
(For Example)

> What you will be doing
> Departure and return times/locations
> Supervision and free-time activities
> Accommodations and curfew times
> How you can be reached by phone

Listed below are some of the activities we have planned to offer to the students during the trip. Initial your approval for your child's involvement in specific activities listed below:
(For Example)

☐ horseback riding   ☐ playing in sports
☐ rock climbing   ☐ swimming in a lake
☐ canoeing   ☐ taking the ropes course
☐ participating in program

Rules of Behavior Expected of Each Student
(For Example)

1. No alcohol or drugs permitted.   4. Follow curfew.
2. Attendance at meetings mandatory.   5. No smoking.
3. No guys in girls' sleeping quarters   6. (as necessary)
   (and vice versa).

Parent Information and Release Form—Page 2

Parent and Student Release Statement:

As parent/legal guardian of *(name of student)*, I have reviewed the information about the youth ministry activity/event and give my permission for the subject of this release to be involved in the overall activities and in the specific activities that I have initialed above.

I/We have reviewed the rules of the activity and agree that the subject of this release will abide by them. I/We also acknowledge that if the subject of the release has to return home early for discipline violations, it will be at my/our expense.

I/We consent to the use of any video images, photographs, audio recordings, or any other visual or audio reproduction that may be taken of the subject of this release during the activity/event to be used, distributed, or shown as *(name of the church or organization)* sees fit.

I/We understand all reasonable safety precautions will be taken at all times by *(name of the church or organization)* and its agents during the events and activities. I/We understand the possibility of unforeseen hazards and know the inherent possibility of risk. I/We agree not to hold *(name of church or organization)*, its leaders, employees, and volunteer staff liable for damages, losses, diseases, or injuries incurred by the subject of this form.

Parent/Guardian Signature _____

Student Signature _____

Date _____ Notarized

Youth Video/Photograph/Tape Release Form

(Name of Church or Youth Ministry)
Youth Video/Photograph/Tape Release Form

(Please Print)

Name of Student _____ Date of Birth _____

Address _____ Age _____

Town _____ State _____ Zip _____

Phone # (____) _____ Sex _____

    I, the undersigned, hereby consent to the use of any video tapes, photo-graphs, slides, audio tapes, or any other visual or audio reproduction by *(name of the organization)* in which I may appear . I understand that these materials may be used for promotion of the youth ministry of *(name of organization)*, including recruitment and fundraising efforts. I release *(name of organization)* from any liability connected with the use of my picture or voice recording as part of any promotion, recruitment, or fundraising program.

Parent/Guardian Signature _____

Student Signature _____
                            (Consented to by Parent/Guardian)

Date _____ Notarized

Volunteer Information Form

(Name of Church or Youth Ministry)
Volunteer Information Form

Dear *(Type Reference Name)*

(Applicant name) has applied for volunteer work with *(name of church or youth ministry)*.

(Name of church or youth ministry) is a Christian program involved with children in trouble or "at risk." The above named is being considered for involvement with a troubled child in a one-to-one relationship or involvement during youth guidance activities. To help us determine whether this person is best suited for this type of volunteer work, we would appreciate you taking the time to answer the questions on this form as fully and specifically as you can. The information received will be kept in confidence.

How long have you known the applicant? _____

In what capacity? _____

Does the applicant have a good home relationship? _____

Does he/she work well with others? _____

Please comment on his/her level of commitment: _____

_____

Does he/she have a tendency to overcommit him/herself? _____

How would you rate him/her according to the following?

	Excellent	Good	Average	Poor	Do Not Know
Personal Habits	☐	☐	☐	☐	☐
Character	☐	☐	☐	☐	☐
Morals	☐	☐	☐	☐	☐
Compassion for Those in Need	☐	☐	☐	☐	☐

Volunteer Information Form — Page 2

	Excellent	Good	Average	Poor	Do Not Know
Responsible to Complete Commitments	☐	☐	☐	☐	☐
Emotional Stability	☐	☐	☐	☐	☐
Christian Maturity	☐	☐	☐	☐	☐
Receives Constructive Criticism Well	☐	☐	☐	☐	☐
Health	☐	☐	☐	☐	☐

If you were in our position, would you, without hesitation, consider this person to be a volunteer with a child/teenager? *(Please explain)*

_____

_____

_____

Is there any reason why you would not recommend this applicant for working with a child? *(Please explain)*

_____

_____

Signature _____ Date _____

Home Phone (____) _____

☐ Please call me, I'd like to give some detailed information concerning this applicant.

Please use the back of this form if more room is needed.

YOUR IMMEDIATE RESPONSE IS GREATLY APPRECIATED!

Accident Report Form

**(Name of Church or Youth Ministry)
Accident Report Form**

(Please Print)

Date of the accident _____ Time of the accident _____

Name of the victim _____ Age of victim _____

Address of victim _____

City _____ State _____ Zip _____

Parent/Guardian of victim _____ Phone (____) _____

Location of accident _____

Names of youth ministry staff leading the activity
(Attach copy of Parent Release Form and Medical Information. List staff, students, or persons who witnessed the accident.)

Name _____ Phone (____) _____

Name _____ Phone (____) _____

Name _____ Phone (____) _____

Describe how the accident happened _____

_____

_____

What were the apparent injuries? _____

_____

Accident Report Form—Page 2

How and by whom were the injuries treated at the scene? _____

_____

_____

What additional medical assistance was sought? _____

_____

_____

What hospital/clinic was used? *(Attach any paperwork stating diagnosis, treatment, and billing.)*

_____

When were parents contacted? By whom? _____

What happened after hospital/clinic treatment? _____

_____

Present condition of victim _____

_____

Name of staff submitting report _____ Date _____